Frank Lloyd Wright

Frank Lloyd Wright at the University of Florida

Frank Lloyd Wright at the University of Florida

Kenneth Treister, FAIA

LibraryPress@UF
Gainesville, Florida

COPYRIGHT

Copyright 2017 by Kenneth Treister.   Book Design by Kenneth Treister.
This work is licensed under a modified Creative Commons Attribution-Noncommercial-No Derivative Works 3.0 Unported License. To view a copy of this license, visit http://creativecommons.org/licenses/by-nc-nd/3.0/. You are free to electronically copy, distribute, and transmit this work if you attribute authorship. However, all printing rights are reserved by the University of Florida Press (http://upress.ufl.edu). Please contact UFP for information about how to obtain copies of the work for print distribution. You must attribute the work in the manner specified by the author or licensor (but not in any way that suggests that they endorse you or your use of the work). For any reuse or distribution, you must make clear to others the license terms of this work. Any of the above conditions can be waived if you get permission from the University Press of Florida. Nothing in this license impairs or restricts the author's moral rights.

ISBN 978-1-944455-05-7 – Cloth
ISBN 978-1-944455-06-4 – Paper

CATALOGING-IN-PUBLICATION DATA

Names: Treister, Kenneth, author | George A. Smathers Libraries, publisher.
Title: Frank Lloyd Wright at the University of Florida / Kenneth Treister, FAIA.
Description: Gainesville, FL : Library Press @ UF, 2016 | Contents: Part I: Two unbuilt fraternity houses, University of Wisconsin and Hanover College–Part II: View from a second perspective, the University of Florida—Part III: The committee, Epitaph-final letter from Mr. Wright—Part IV: Renderings of the Zeta Beta Tau House. | Summary: An account of architect Frank Lloyd Wright's connections with the University of Florida and his design for the Zeta Beta Tau fraternity house at the University.
Subjects: LCSH: Wright, Frank Lloyd, 1867-1959. | Treister, Kenneth. | University of Florida. | Architecture—Designs and plans. | Greek letter societies—Florida—Gainesville—History. | Zeta Beta Tau (Fraternity).
Classification: NA737.W7T74 2016

PICTURE & ILLUSTRATION CREDITS

Unless otherwise cited, all photographs and graphics are by Kenneth Treister.

Thanks to M. Jeffrey Baker, for six floor plans and nine renderings illustrating Frank Lloyd Wright's design for the ZBT Fraternity House for the University of Florida, included with permissions. Thanks to The Frank Lloyd Wright Foundation Archives (The Museum of Modern Art | Avery Architectural & Fine Arts Library, Columbia University), for the photographs, included with permissions: Wright at 88 (1955), Wright at the dinner (1937), Frank Lloyd Wright and his wife Olgivanna (1951), Frank Lloyd Wright with Mr. and Mrs. Yofan, and Taliesin West with "tabby" stone walls.

Thanks to Hanover College, for the photograph of Hanover College, included with permissions.

Thanks to the University of Florida Archives, for the architectural drawings of the ZBT Fraternity House for the University of Florida, photographs of Century Tower & University Auditorium, the Florida Gym, and Tigert Hall (the administration building), University of Florida, Gainesville, included with permissions.

PUBLISHER

First published in the United States of America in 2016 by the LIBRARY PRESS @ UF, an imprint of the UF Press and George A. Smathers Libraries, Judith Russell, Dean, Univesrity of Florida, 535 Library West, PO Box 117000 Gainesville FL 32611-7000

DEDICATION

This book is dedicated to the memory of the late Kalvin Platt, a member of the small group of young architectural students at the University of Florida who in 1951 brought Frank Lloyd Wright to Gainesville. Kalvin went on to an illustrious international career in landscape architecture, planning and urban design.

ACKNOWLEDGMENTS

I want to acknowledge: Judith Russell, Dean of the Smathers Libraries, University of Florida, her staff and particularly Laurie Taylor, John Nemmers and Barbara Hood for their enthusiastic and scholarly study of Florida history and the history of the University of Florida that made this publication a reality; Martha Kohen, University of Florida Professor; the editing skills of Ves Spindler, Marsden Brooks and Cindy Turner; Indira Berndtson, Administrator, Historic Studies Frank Lloyd Wright Archives and Margo Stipe, Curator and Registrar of Collections, Frank Lloyd Wright Archives, while the main credit for this story goes back to 1951 when Frank Lloyd Wright, the world's most renowned architect, accepted the commission to design a fraternity house for Zeta Beta Tau (ZBT); Nils Schweizer, Wright's Florida representative; Eugene Masselink, Wright's personal secretary; William Wesley Peters, Wright's project captain; Dr. Ludd M. Spivey, President, Florida Southern College who gave advice and council; George Baughman, Business Manager of the University of Florida for his guidance; the brothers of the ZBT Fraternity, which Frank Lloyd Wright affectionately called "The Fraternity Boys"; and particularly the small group of architectural students, classmates of the author, who were brave enough to think beyond their provincial status and bring light to the University of Florida and the School of Architecture and Allied Arts: Tim Siebert, Kalvin Platt, William Ruff, Earl Starnes, Joseph Rentscher, Erick Meyerhoff, Robert Gunn, Robin John, Ernest Daffin, Newton Sayers, Joan Warriner, Ken Warriner, Charles Crumpton, Raymond Dinklage, Alfred Leland Fisher, Sheldon Gans, Richard Levine, Paul Reiner, Jerry Kurth, Jim Casey and Alan Borg; and to my wife Helyne, who has been my lifetime inspiration.

CONTENTS

PART I - TWO UNBUILT FRATERNITY HOUSES   1 UNIVERSITY OF WISCONSIN AND HANOVER COLLEGE

PART II - VIEW FROM A SECOND PERSPECTIVE   11 THE UNIVERSITY OF FLORIDA

PART III - THE COMMITTEE   27

EPITAPH - FINAL LETTER FROM MR. WRIGHT   49

PART IV - RENDERINGS OF THE ZETA BETA TAU (ZBT) HOUSE   50

APPENDIX - LETTERS BY AUTHOR TO MR. WRIGHT   65 ARCHITECTURAL PLANS, AND NEWSPAPER ARTICLES PHOTOGRAPH OF ZBT FRATERNITY

FRANK LLOYD WRIGHT AT
THE UNIVERSITY OF FLORIDA

The curtain opens on the sad story of the legendary architect Frank Lloyd Wright and the University of Florida. It begins with great expectations and ends with a great loss. This story can be told from three distant perspectives, all at universities . . . years and worlds apart.

PART I — TWO UNBUILT FRATERNITY HOUSES

UNIVERSITY OF WISCONSIN — 1924

The first perspective is from a series of events that occurred over years in the creative world of Frank Lloyd Wright, arguably the world's greatest contemporary architect. The second is a series of events in the early '50s in Gainesville, Florida, the home of the University of Florida . . . seemingly worlds apart.

Let us first tell the story from the work of Frank Lloyd Wright at the University of Wisconsin. The year was 1924 and Mr. Wright was bathing in the glory of the recent opening and success of his Imperial Hotel in Tokyo, Japan, a most impressive architectural achievement of worldwide importance.

At this time Richard Lloyd Jones, the former editor and publisher of the Wisconsin State Journal and a cousin of Mr. Wright's was a member of the alumni board of the Mu chapter of Phi Gamma Delta Fraternity at the University of Wisconsin, in Madison.

The fraternity wanted a new fraternity house, and Mr. Jones suggested that Frank Lloyd Wright would be the perfect choice. So Wright was selected and designed a most beautiful home for the fraternity, one that carried on the traditions of Wright's Textile Block Houses he had recently successfully designed and built in Southern California.

The massing of the home, particularly the front façade, was reminiscent of Wright's admiration for the architecture of the pre-Colombian Mayan civilization that flourished centuries earlier in Mesoamerica. Mayan architecture has had a strong influence on the legendary work of Frank Lloyd Wright. Although Frank Lloyd Wright during his lifetime and in his voluminous writings said he only admired Mayan architecture—he always denied using any of the Mayan architectural forms or details, probably due to his immense ego, pride of ownership, and the modern ideal that it's against some mythical moral code to copy or be influenced by anything of the past. Nevertheless, Wright copied and was inspired greatly, particularly by the design concepts of the massing, shapes, horizontality and stone construction techniques of the Maya.

The front façade of the Mu House was a combination of strong horizontal and vertical lines set into exposed concrete block. There is a solidity and permanence to the front façade that softens as it tapers off to the lake front of Lake Mendota. This rear mass was to be horizontal and was used to house the student sleeping and studying wing.

There was to be a roof deck on top for the fraternity brothers to enjoy the beautiful views of Lake Mendota. Unfortunately this fraternity house was never built. A study of the front façade elements reveals a interesting use of variable masses as a play on volume, voids and texture to create a work of architectonic sculpture. The elements are at juxtaposition to each other and are not perfectly but randomly symmetrical. This design element is relatively unique in the work of Frank Lloyd Wright and perhaps would have become a prototype for Wright to elaborate on in the future—if the design had been executed.

In their book *Frank Lloyd Wright In His Renderings 1887–1959*, Yukio Futagawa and Bruce Brooks Pfeiffer discusses this unbuilt project:

> "And another concrete block structure: this one was planned for a Madison Wisconsin. In the case other colder climate to fit this is the block walls were constructed so as to provide for necessary installation the tall mast at the edge of the hill contains the public rooms, lounge and dining, while the winning reach back provides for student dormitories."

The Phi Gamma Delta Fraternity House
Frank Lloyd Wright, Architect
University of Wisconsin, Madison
1924

Parker Auditorium
Hanover College

HANOVER COLLEGE, 1941

Then the year flashes forward to 1941 when Mr. Wright again designs another fraternity house, this one at Hanover College in Hanover, Indiana. It was to be called "The Walter L. Fisher, Memorial Chapter House, Chi of Sigma Chi, Hanover Indiana." This was the second fraternity house by Frank Lloyd Wright of the trio of what would unfortunately become an unbuilt fraternity houses.

It is relevant to understand that Hanover College, founded in 1827, is situated on 650 acres of land overlooking the Ohio River, a site with climbing paths, cliffs and views of the Ohio River from three different bends in the river. The campus, considered one of the Nation's most scenic, is characterized by its harmonious Georgian-styled architecture. Based on this, in 1941 the college turned down Wright's plan to rebuild the Sigma Chi (ΣX) fraternity house because, in their opinion, it did not match the tranquility of the existing Georgian architecture. Here is the paradox. The Sigma Chi house, as designed, would become the prototype for the Zeta Beta Tau (ZBT) house years later at the University of Florida. The two designs were similar with the major difference being that the Hanover design was not as well situated into the landscape or as gracious; its proportions were not as refined and the massing not as homogeneous and flowing as the one he would later design for the University of Florida.

The Sigma Chi house, like the Zeta Beta Tau house that followed, had a grand Social Hall with floor to ceiling glass wall and doors opening onto a large circular recreation terrace. However, this terrace was level with the ground and not elevated (like the Zeta Beta Tau House in Gainesville would have been) with the battered circular masonry wall rising out of the hill. It seems with time and a second opportunity to refine the design, Wright's ZBT house is by far the more beautiful of the two. The dream of any architect is to be able to design a building a second time, correcting, modifying and perfecting its form and spirit.

AN INTERESTING PARADOX

Frank Lloyd Wright, during his life, championed the cause against the "International Style" of European, modernistic architecture. He felt it cold and inhuman, not gently organic or natural in harmony with man and his senses. Hanover College also wanted a campus with these qualities, qualities they felt were found in their traditional Georgian architecture. However, Hanover also thought that Wright's style was unsympathetic to their taste, particularly for an institution of higher learning. Yet these two allies in this ongoing struggle against International Style modernism could not come to terms with an acceptable home design that would suit both their puritanical tastes. The Sigma Chi house was never built. Perhaps the ZBT design, which was more gracious and beautiful, would have pleased Hanover College more.

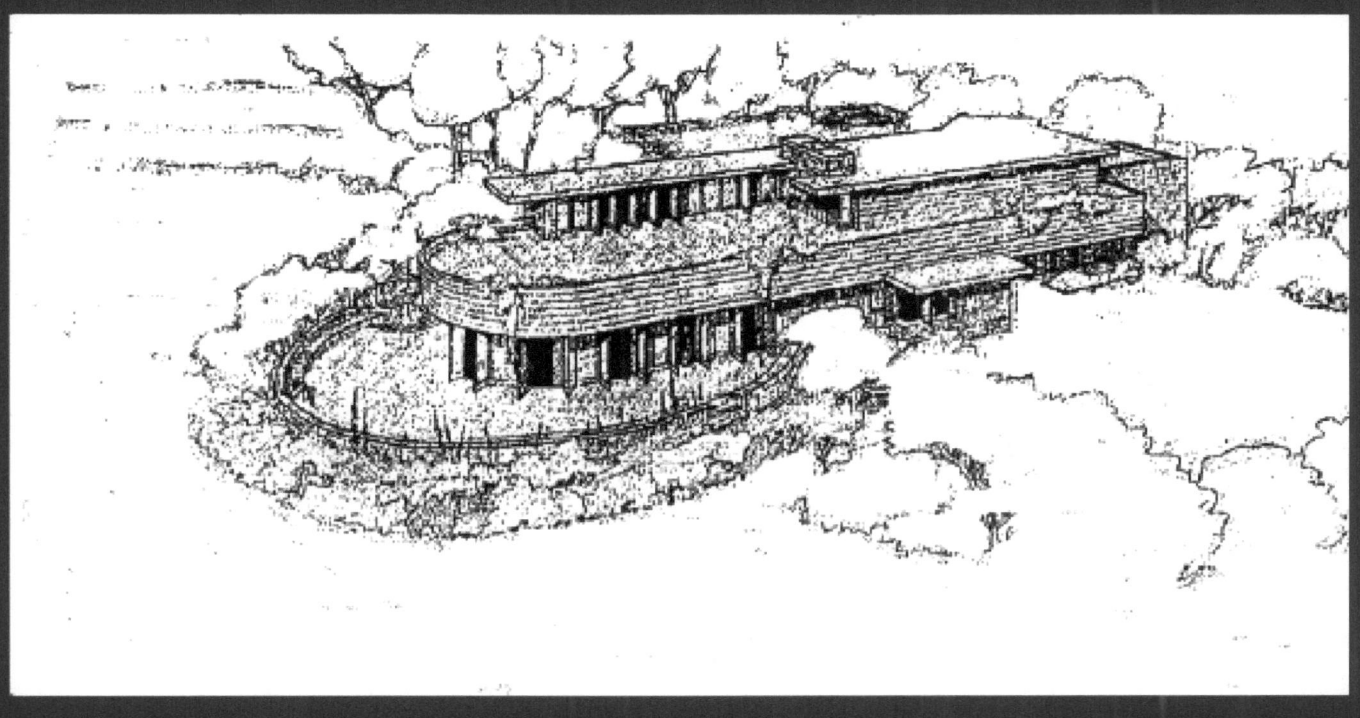

The Sigma Chi House
Frank Lloyd Wright, Architect
Hanover College, Hanover, Indiana
1941

THE WALTER L FISHER MEMORIAL CHAPTER HOUSE
CHI OF SIGMA CHI   HANOVER INDIANA
FRANK LLOYD WRIGHT ARCHITECT

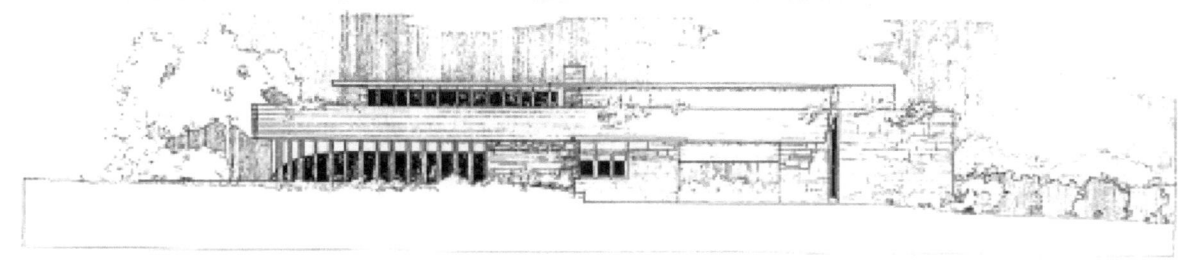

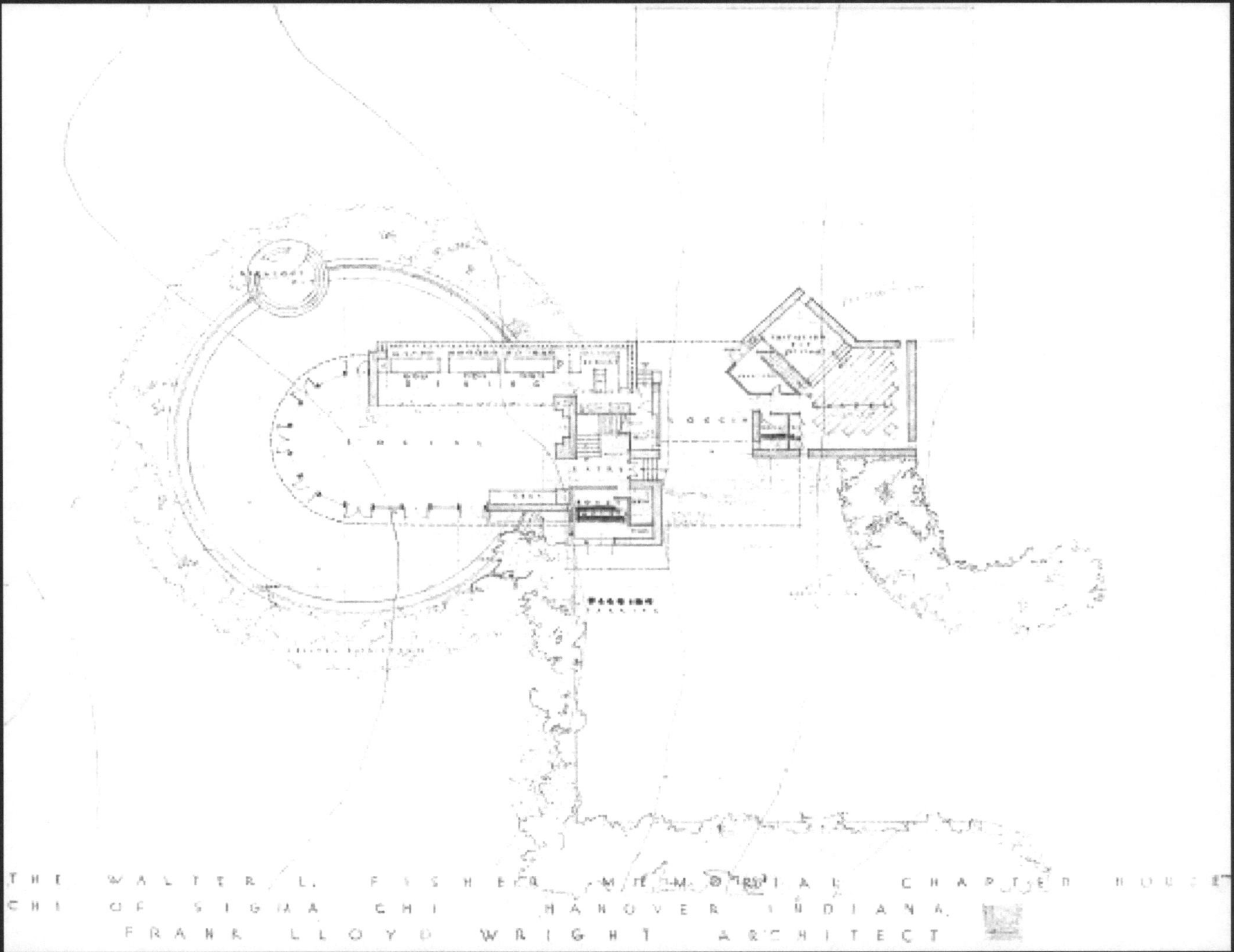

THE WALTER L. FISHER MEMORIAL CHAPTER HOUSE
CHI OF SIGMA CHI HANOVER INDIANA
FRANK LLOYD WRIGHT ARCHITECT

THE WALTER L. FISHER MEMORIAL CHAPTER HOUSE
CHI OF SIGMA CHI HANOVER INDIANA
FRANK LLOYD WRIGHT ARCHITECT

Tower & Auditorium
University of Florida, Gainesville

PART II — VIEW FROM A SECOND PERSPECTIVE

THE UNIVERSITY OF FLORIDA — 1951

Then, once again, we flash forward over 10 years to the Gainesville campus of the University of Florida. The year was 1951.

•

In his beautiful book *Treasures of Taliesin, Seventy-Six Unbuilt Designs*[1], Bruce Brooks Pfeiffer, Director of Frank Lloyd Wright's Archives, discussing the ZBT Fraternity House at the University of Florida and the circumstances surrounding it, explaining what went wrong with the deadly "committee" and why it was not built.

"Wright designed three fraternity houses during his career, in 1924, 1941, and the Zeta Beta Tau Fraternity House in 1952. None was ever built. Although each of the three differed from the others in materials employed, site, and location, one design feature was common to all three: each contained a large two- or three-story living room to serve as a great hall at one end of the building, with dormitory bedrooms stretching out behind it. In the case of the Zeta Beta Tau House, the great hall gives onto a large circular outdoor terrace for dining and entertainment.

The project progressed as far as the working drawing stage, but the clients were a committee—a deadly situation especially where creative work is concerned. A committee, Wright once said, functions like a jury selection. First they throw out the worst; then they throw out the best; then they settle on the middle ground as being the safest. The factor of safety, Dankmar Adler once insisted, becomes frequently a factor of ignorance. How often it was that much that is the best of Wright's work was not built simply because of this factor."

---

1 Bruce Brooks Pfeiffer. *Treasures of Taliesin: Seventy-Seven Unbuilt Designs*. Rohnert Park, CA: Pomegranate Communications, 1999, page 115

ZETA BETA TAU ON FRATERNITY ROW

In 1951, I was a third-year student in a five-year course of study in architecture at the University of Florida. I had joined Zeta Beta Tau Fraternity when I was a freshman at the University of Miami and, when I transferred in 1949, became active in their chapter at the University of Florida. Our fraternity house was on the busy, commercial University Avenue in an old wooden home, in many ways a charming house—like so many fraternity houses in Gainesville were. At this time the University announced in the student paper, *The Florida Alligator*, that a beautiful wooded site on campus would soon be opened for a new fraternity row, like the custom so many other Universities had. Our fraternity, which was relatively small and new on campus, was, therefore, interested in building a new fraternity house for the allure of a new home—on what should be a proper fraternity on-campus environment was a very inviting idea. Being an architectural student, the fraternity appointed me to be in charge of this unfolding venture.

•

George Baughman was the Business Manager of the University at the time and in many ways was more powerful than the University President. The president was the ceremonial head, set long-term policy, met alumni and raised funds, but the true power was in the spending and allocating of those funds—and that job was in George's hands. He had a grand and spacious office in the old Administration Building, soon to be replaced by a new building being built at the time on 13th Street, near the entrance to the University.

I had previously met George Baughman but was surprised when one day he invited me to visit him in his office. He started by telling me that he had heard ZBT was interested in building a new fraternity house on the proposed "fraternity row." He then told me that the Federal Government, through the Housing and Home Finance Agency, was soon to pass a bill that would make fraternities eligible for Federal funds allocated as student dormitories. His message was simple. He was an alumni and board member of a prominent local fraternity, and they also were delirious about building a fraternity house on the new fraternity row and applying for the Federal housing funds. Since he was in such a prominent position at the University, he did not want to be the first to apply since all applications went through his desk. He had no problem being the second to apply. Could he help us with our project and put us down as the first to apply? I, of course, said yes, we would be delighted and would welcome his help. Unfortunately as you will see as the story unfolds, we had other problems and never got to this final stage of finance.

THE LECTURE

The University of Florida's School of Architecture & Allied Arts, headed at the time by Dean William T. Arnett, had a prohibition, one of many, of guest lecturers. If anyone were going to address the students, it would be a member of the faculty. Not a very happy prospect for students eager to learn a broad understanding of the vast world of architecture, the mother of all arts.

Some of us (architectural students in our class) had just returned with glowing reports from a student architectural conference on the architectural education at North Carolina State University in Raleigh, a good architectural school at the time. One of the most interesting items was the excellent guest-lecturers that often visited their campus. We were rebels and had to continuously fight for an education at Gainesville while they seemed to have everything given to them on a silver platter. The interesting thing was that when we told of our adventures in trying to make a poor school better, they said they wanted to transfer for the excitement of our struggle.

One night, while discussing what we considered another nonsensical University rule, we sat around in our Common Room and played a "What-If" game. If we could invite anyone we wanted to come and give us a lecture . . . who would that be? Being students of architecture, there was really only one choice if we were going to shoot for the stars, Frank Lloyd Wright, America's, perhaps the world's, greatest living architect. So we had the president of the Student Chapter of the AIA, Ernest Daffin, write Mr. Wright inviting him to lecture to the University of Florida students, (independent of the architectural faculty) and much to our astonishment, he accepted!

By the time Frank Lloyd Wright arrived, word that the internationally-acclaimed architect would be visiting our campus created a level of excitement usually reserved for a University football game against a hated opponent, of which Florida had several.

The small, commercial, twin-engine plane arrived, and the gangway was rolled out and positioned so the passengers could disembark. Then, larger than life, Mr. Wright, silhouetted against the black opening and struck a pose. Immaculately dressed in a dark suit, the master of Taliesin, with flowing cape, a jaunty beret and holding an elegant walking stick, descended the steps.

About twenty of us, all from our class, were waiting just inside the entrance of the terminal. The members of the faculty, those that never missed a chance to belittle the work of Wright, had formed an honor guard flanking the bottom of the stairs on the tarmac, one Mr. Wright would have to pass through. We were all watching sheepishly as he descended to approach the first members of the faculty who had their hands held out to greet him.

Looking neither left or right, he walked right by them, leaving in his tiny wake, stunned, open-mouthed professors who thought they should be shown the highest level of respect. It was great! This characteristically rude behavior on his part, the result of our having cautioned him that guest lecturers—even the great one—were not welcome at our school.

Inside the terminal, Mr. Wright greeted us all warmly. My God! There he was, Frank Lloyd Wright, shaking hands with us! It was a moment none of us would ever forget.

By this time in his already legendary career, Frank Lloyd Wright had left his indelible mark on the world of architecture by establishing a lifetime of humanistic achievement, an exquisite exhibition of his design genius.

We had reserved one of the finest rooms (with a sitting room as requested) in the Thomas Hotel, built in 1910 and at the time the best, well really, the only suitable hotel in Gainesville for our esteemed guest. The only other accommodations for a visitor to this small college town would have been the typical semi-circular row of small bungalows called motels. Wright was with us for three unforgettable days, using the lobby lounge of the hotel as an impromptu lecture hall.

Before his lecture Frank Lloyd Wright agreed to speak to our small student group that had invited him to Gainesville during two informal talks.

It was beautiful. Our small group sitting in rapt attention as a true genius talked to us in simple conversation. Here in this small, mostly rural, Southern college town—in a traditional Classic Revival wooden hotel with wide, white veranda out front—were a group of neophyte architectural students sitting in overstuffed, slightly musty lounge chairs in the lobby, listening to the modern master of world architecture.

Since he did not want to enter the Architecture building but instructed us on a second occasion to assemble outside on a verdant grass area under a large tree. We sat on the ground in a semicircle and Wright, with Olgivana at his side, stood on a small rise above us in his hallmark cape and porkpie hat. He gave us a lecture on architecture that was inspiring and very memorable in the setting under the tree. The only exposure to the faculty was at a short lunch they had set up at the hotel the day after the lecture.

We had reserved the Florida Gymnasium for October 23, 1951, posted posters, printed a small pamphlet, and sold tickets around campus to come hear the legendary Frank Lloyd Wright speak. It was standing room only, estimated at about 5,000, and the sale of tickets at $1.00 for adult admission and $.75 for students brought in enough for us to pay Mr. Wright's standard lecture fee of $1,000, plus expenses. Mr. Wright's lecture was described the next day in the Jacksonville Florida *Times Union* article with the headline "States' Rights Return Urged by Architect as Frank Lloyd Wright Raps Unionism, Centralization of Government." An unattributed article, probably in the *Gainesville Sun*, said "Wright Declares Europeans Look Upon U.S. as Dollar Imperialists." Both headlines underline Wright's belief in decentralization, as echoed in his agrarian concept for Broad Acre City, less central government, and a return to an American architecture free of ties to the rage for contemporary European International Style architecture, a rage that still exists.

NEWSPAPER ACCOUNTS OF WRIGHT'S LECTURE

For clarification, the following is from three articles on Frank Lloyd Wright's speech at the University of Florida on Tuesday, October 23, 1951

Article, *Gainesville Sun* — Saturday, October 20, 1951

Wright delights, shocks audience in Atlanta talk

ATLANTA — Frank Lloyd Wright, the snappy, 82-year-old dean of modern architecture, both delighted and shocked a large audience at Georgia Tech last night. The philosophical discussion of the 82-year-old Wright touched, at times, only vaguely on architecture and often had more bite than design. He dubbed designing as the blind spot in American culture and added that we know a great deal more about everything else than we do about it.

"All you need as proof," he said, "is to look at the buildings in which our educational campaigns are carried out."

Then he touched on politics, the state of the world, capitalism, the "newly rich," the United Nations and education.

Of the latter he said simply: "Education has not been on speaking terms with culture for a long time." On the American people as a whole: "They sit behind the wheel of their car with a cigar cocked at 45 degrees and their hat pulled down over their eyes thinking they're 125 horsepower."

And finally of the American architecture: "We've got the kind of architecture we deserve. We did it. It wasn't done to us. We just didn't know any better."

Article, *Gainesville Sun* — Tuesday, October 23, 1951

Wright to talk here tonight

Frank Lloyd Wright is well known throughout the country for his impromptu speeches covering a wide variety of subjects, and the 82-year-old father of modern architecture is expected to deliver one of those talks here tonight.

Wright is appearing at the University of Florida under the sponsorship of the student chapter of the American Institute of Architects. He will speak in the University gymnasium at 8 p.m.

Speeches by Wright, which are rare occasions, cover a wide variety of subjects ranging from music and cookery to posing for photographers. His "off-the-cuff" style of delivery usually keeps his audience well amused and sometimes confused, but always entertained.

Wright is the famed designer of some of the most controversial architectural projects throughout the world. The foremost example of his style of design in Florida is Florida Southern College at Lakeland. He also designed the ultramodern Johnson Wax Co. plant and the Imperial Hotel in Tokyo.

Article, *Gainesville Sun* — Wednesday, October 24, 1951

WRIGHT DECLARES
Europeans look upon U.S. as 'dollar imperialists'

By Jim Camp

People in other countries think of the United States as a nation of "dollar imperialists," famed architect Frank Lloyd Wright said last night.

Speaking before an attentive audience of around 5,000 in Florida Gymnasium, the "father of American architecture" pointed out that those abroad don't like the Marshall Plan.

"They think it is a scheme to buy Europe away from the Communists, " Wright said, basing his conclusions on personal observations during a recent trip overseas.

"They resent the fact that we think they can be bought—but they took our money!" the salty, 81-year-old proponent of "organic architecture" stated.

Defining organic architecture as "living, natural architecture," Wright simplified his meaning by pointing out that organic "things" are the only "living things."

The South, Wright insisted, can go straight to organic architecture if we will rid ourselves of "Colonial" styling and other sentimentalities.

Colonial architecture was dismissed as "bastardized Greek." Following the Civil War, the speaker reminded the South did not go in for other such "extravagances" as skyscrapers, which he said will eventually have to be torn down.

In spite of all their opportunities, Americans have developed no culture of their own, Wright said, but have remained a nation of imitators. Our "style" of architecture, he added, has been the "blind spot" on any sort of culture we may have attempted.

Cultural development, according to Wright, must now come from the hearts of the people—the democratic family unit—since education hasn't waked up."

De-centralization will be the salvation of the nation, if it is to have a culture of its own," Wright stated. "We point to our skyscrapers with the greatest pride, yet the country is the best place to build a skyscraper."

"The Russians know this."

The American unions have put the country on the assembly line "for keeps," Wright pointed out, but they must be made to realize that they can't kill off apprenticeship and live.

"We must do something about it," he warned, "or we will have a 'machine architecture' of prefabrication, home-wiring and other things we are being driven to by the unions."

Stressing the need of a good atmosphere in which to live, Wright said the pursuit of the beautiful is the only pursuit of America, as a democracy, that is worth a man's time.

"All the fine words in our language have been sold down the river by the advertising agencies," stated Wright. He challenged anyone in the audience to state his chief interest in life, as an American.

When someone expressed a desire to be able to "think freely," Wright attached by asking, "How about "living freely?" to spontaneous applause. Of the "Four Freedoms," the speaker charged that if America has to count its freedoms by fours, then we don't really have freedom.

Comparing government to architecture in a structural sense, Wright said that if we do not have a good structure of government then we can't live happily. "We must get the idea over to Americans that we are somebody in our right," he insisted.

Declaring frankly, that "architecture is in a worse pickle than painting." Wright went on to say that sculpture, as a great art, has disappeared from the face of the earth.

"Music is the only one of the great arts remaining," the architect said, "and that is because it is still modern, having been based upon instruments that we continue to use."

Renewing his attack on Colonial building, Wright explained that people tend to love this kind of thing because they refuse to live in the present—which, he said, has more to offer.

Organic architecture, he said, still refusing to give ground to any other style, produces buildings, which become part of their surroundings.

"You don't have to go to a little hole in the wall to see them either!" he pointed out.

Article, *Florida Times Union* — Jacksonville, Florida, Wednesday, October 24, 1951

States' Rights Return Urged By Architect
Frank Lloyd Wright Rape Unionism, Centralizing of Government

In a speech on the University of Florida campus tonight, the "father of modern architecture," Frank Lloyd Wright, advocated the return of states' rights and decentralization of government, and at the same time hit at unionism and the nation's educational system.

In calling for States' rights, he said democracy needs sound structure in Government, that the Constitution was such an organic structure but has constantly been changed by having this taken away from it.

He deplored the fact that the unions in America have thrown the trades out of line and has put itself on the assembly line by limiting apprenticeship.

The 81-year-old architect stated "we have no culture in this country. It is up to the young architects to change this, since the environment in which we live is the very basis for a culture.

"Neither is education doing anything about it. It will have to come from the family at home," he told a large crowd at Florida Gymnasium.

As advocate of organic architecture over the colonial type, Wright said the South can go straight to organic architecture because it was defeated in the Civil War and did not go in for "such extravagances like skyscrapers which will have to be torn down."

He also gave a boost to Dr. Ludd M. Spivey, president of Florida Southern College, who was in attendance tonight. Wright said the FSC campus was an attempt at an organic architecture for the young.

Wright himself designed many of the buildings on the Florida Southern Campus.

Above is the Historic Florida Gymnasium, where Frank Lloyd Wright delivered his important lecture on Tuesday, October 23, 1951, a lecture that gave rise to his design of the Zeta Beta Tau Fraternity House.

WRIGHT LECTURE AND RUSSIA

This brings to mind a strange anachronism that came to light during Wright's talk at the University of Florida. Frank Lloyd Wright in his Gainesville lecture restated three of his lifelong philosophic concepts: One, his disdain for strong central government stating instead his belief in State's Rights and, therefore, the regionalism he displayed in his work; second, his dislike for unionism; and third, his life-long campaign against both imported traditional and the so-called European International Style architecture.

The hypothesis of our country's regionalism was to express the nation's democratic soul, the "soul of America," as a region with a unique concept of freedom. Regionalists, as they were called, basically championed Midwestern values and work ethnic, the same value system promulgated by Frank Lloyd Wright, with his traditional roots in Wisconsin. For the mid-section of the country provided the distance needed by the Regionalists to be physically apart from the natural European influences that prevailed along the Eastern Seaboard, particularly in its thriving immigrant cities.

It is strange Wright was the main guest speaker at the First All-Union Congress of Soviet Architects in Russia during the height of Joseph Stalin's power. During his talks there he praised the Soviet System even though it was the epitome of centralized government: a communist government controlled by unionism and sponsor of the International Comintern (The International Department of the Central Committee of the Communist Party of the Soviet Union), the aspiring centralized government of the world.

Wright wrote at the time an article in "Izvestia" the Russian government's mass circulation newspaper where he championed his call for organic architecture as opposed to the popular "International Style" which is still so popular in the West today: ". . . Unfortunately most of those buildings inspired by the European left wing in modern architecture are ugly structures badly built because no architect of the lift wing is really enough of a technician to build original buildings. Some of these architects are painters experimenting with building as they would with any genre. So it is maybe difficult now for the Russian people to understand that the new Simplicity of organic architecture does not mean plainness . . ."[2]

2 Frank Lloyd Wright Quarterly, Fall 1993, Vol. 4 No 4, p 8.

In addition the strange love affair is perplexing since Russia at the time was a country brutally controlled by Joseph Stalin, whose taste was pure European tinsel architecture as witness by his orchestrated Moscow subway stations of dripping chandeliers and gold-gilded walls. The only sense one could make of this strange alliance of opposites in Mr. Wright's mind was that they had a common enemy — the International Style of architecture. "The enemy of your enemy is your friend."

In addition, one might surmise that Wright's Russian wife, Olgivanna (his third), who went with him to Russia and cast a strong spell over the architect, might have had some affect in his flirtation with the Soviet Union. Perhaps his strong ego might also have influenced him in this inner conflict of ideas, as well as his pride when this powerful country's architects, invited him, dined him and praised him at their First Congress, an honor he was not afforded at that time by the American architectural fraternity.[3]

Back in Gainesville in the early 1950s, I had the only car in our small architectural class at the time of Wright's visit, an old Buick convertible, so it fell on me to be Mr. Wright's chauffer and guide during his visit, a duty I relished. There I was, a 20-year-old student of architecture, riding around Gainesville with the most acclaimed architect of our time! I also had this honor some time later when Richard Neutra (the famous Austrian, then American architect) visited the school. It seems that Mr. Wright's visit opened the gates to allow other architects of note to visit our college.

One afternoon, October 23 to be exact, because he made it so easy to feel comfortable in his presence, I got up the nerve to ask if he would consider designing our fraternity house. I was a member of Zeta Beta Tau Fraternity, having joined originally when I attended the University of Miami for my freshman year. He agreed, on one condition: That the architectural students would take an active part in the building construction. I quickly agreed.

Mr. Wright had a standard fee for this service as well: A flat 10% of the project's cost. In our case, that came to $10,000 since the ultimate construction budget was $100,000. We went to our families and others to raise the money. We managed to raise quite a lot, but not enough. No matter. Mr. Wright moved ahead on his design.

---

3 *Frank Lloyd Wright In His Renderings 1887–1959*. By Yukio Futagawa and Bruce Brooks Pfeiffer, A.D.A. Edita, Tokyo, 1984. The Fellowship, Roger Friedland & Harold Zellman, Harper Collins, New York, 2006, page 315

Based on the fact he and I had spent a short but intense time together, we had formed a nice relationship. I was to act as the intermediary between Mr. Wright, the fraternity, and the University and its Building Committee. Unfortunately the Building Committee was made up of small-minded bureaucrats who seemed to love the power they had in the building process, particularly when pitted against a world famous architect from another part of the country—another world, another place in time. So the sad note is that I graduated and entered the Navy in 1953 before the project could be realized. Once my work as a filter between Wright and the committee was over, the two could not agree on almost any front and the project fell into acrimony, resulting in a great loss for the fraternity, the University of Florida, and architecture.

Wright at the dinner for the First All-Union Congress of Soviet Architects, 1937.
Wright and his wife, Olgivanna, are in the left center just below the standing waiter. An unidentified gentleman is seated between them.

Frank Lloyd Wright and his wife Olgivanna as they disembark from an Air France plane in May 1951, upon arrival in Italy.

Frank Lloyd Wright is talking with Mr. and Mrs. Yofan at the Society of Cultural Relations Banquet in Moscow. Mr. Yofan was the architect for the proposed Palace of the Soviets.

The Administration Building at the University of Florida, Gainesville.

PART III — THE COMMITTEE

"TELL THE PROFESSORS…"

There was a constant flow of letters during 1951 and 1952 between Frank Lloyd Wright, his office, and myself. I evolved into the representative of the fraternity and architect in dealing with the University. The letters I sent were all addressed to Mr. Wright but many were answered by his long-time secretary and apprentice, Eugene Masselink. The letters that came directly from Wright were always extremely brief and to the point, one or two sentences. They were always on his beautiful, small, beige stationary, typed in landscape format in brown ink, with his red square, Frank Lloyd Wright's symbol taken from the traditional Japanese seal. They were classic.

The correspondence that was the most critical and confrontational concerned presumed code violations found by the State Board of Control's architect, Guy C. Fulton, and the University committee in charge of reviewing and approving the plans. In August 1952 George Baughman notified the 10 fraternities applying to locate on Fraternity Row at the time that the control of the projects would pass from the fraternities' control to that of the Board of Control Architect (Guy C. Fulton) and a University committee.

That University committee found 22 issues of nonconformity when they reviewed Wright's preliminary drawings for the ZBT house. What follows are the areas where they said the plans did not meet their minimum code requirements.

THE CODE — THE BUREAUCRAT'S BIBLE

Unfortunately architectural building codes abandon common sense, logic, and good design principles and rely instead on bureaucratic and arbitrary written rules that in reality often make no sense at all. This phenomenon was described in an interesting book that I read years ago that covered the abandonment of common sense in our bureaucratic and politically-correct society.

There were three main issues that plagued the ZBT house at Gainesville and ultimately defeated the work. Two related items were the budget and the connected issue of Mr. Wright's and the architectural student's desire to work on the construction of the actual building, thereby reducing the cost of construction while educating the students at the same time.

The third was code violations which Frank Lloyd Wright characterized as "the only obstacle are these criticisms from the University." At one point Wright sarcastically referred to the committee and said "It is a real pleasure to soothe the fears of the University experts. Herewith the answers."

Let me discuss the two code disputes that stand out most clearly in my memory as typical of the kind of obstructions the University put in Mr. Wright's path. Perhaps it was small-minded state bureaucrats enjoying criticizing America's greatest architect. The committee is long gone and the members, I am sure, have forgotten the negative meetings, but their legacy is that the University of Florida does not have an architectural work of Frank Lloyd Wright on its campus, a work which would have been a wonderful educational example and important attraction on campus.

THE SETBACK ISSUE

The site had typical American front, rear, and side arbitrary setbacks. Each side setback of 10', if followed, would leave an alley or tunnel between two adjoining structures of 20', a narrow space too small for proper landscaping, giving both neighbors limited privacy of sight and sound, disrespectful to both, although this would have been approved under the stated guidelines at the time. Mr. Wright's more respectful solution would have placed the ZBT House at an angle so that the space between neighbors would be a triangle allowing proper space, landscape, and privacy. It was rejected by the committee.

On the next page are two simple drawings. The first shows the code specified 10' side setbacks, which are actually disrespectful of the neighbor. The second shows Wright's brilliant solution for the ZBT house, which graciously respected its neighboring house.

SET BACKS

BY CODE – DISRESPECTFUL

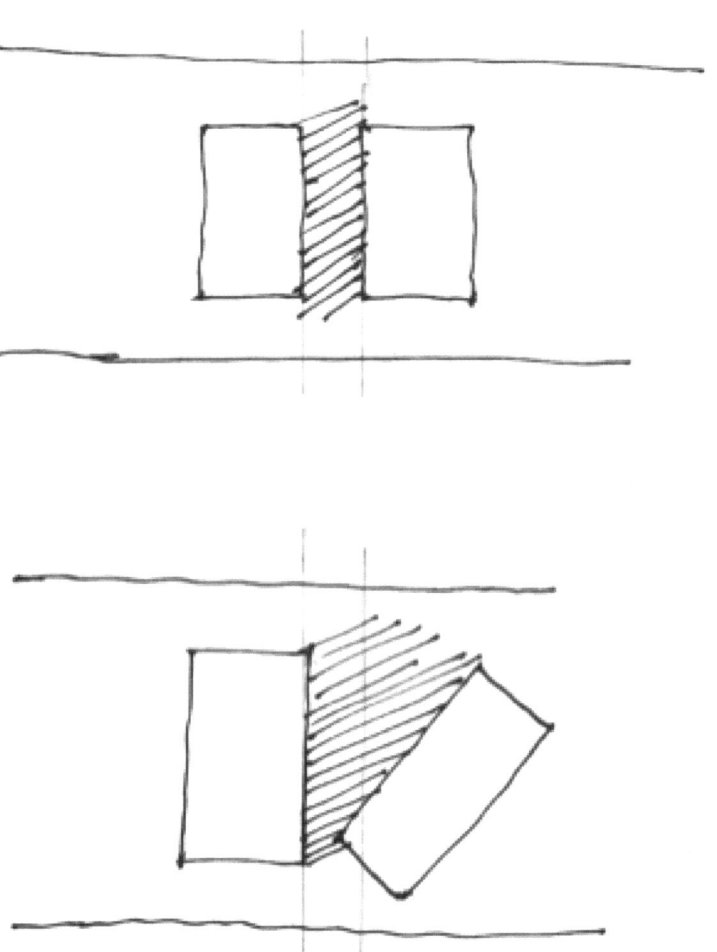

BY FRANK LLOYD WRIGHT – RESPECTFUL

BY TILTING THE HOUSE AND VIOLATING THE SET BACK IN ONE SMALL CORNER BOTH NEIGHBORS HAVE MORE SPACE TO ENJOY

This rendering shows the close proximity of the open balcony and the ground… a solution that Frank Lloyd Wright envisioned as the second emergency fire escape.

THE FIRE ESCAPE ISSUE

A second code violation that the University committee raised was the fact that the house had only one fire stair from its second and third floor. Frank Lloyd Wright usually places the central stair and the fireplace mass in the center of his homes as a fulcrum from which the house was balanced on either side.

I remember clearly his letter, which started: "tell the professors that any healthy college student can jump off the rear terrace and land safely on his feet." I, of course, did not read the letter as it was written when I appeared before the Committee but said something to the effect . . . "Dear Gentleman: I respectful request that you consider the slopped site and the fact that the upper terrace, which opens from the bedrooms, is only about 8' or so from the ground and in an emergency provides another safe and easy exit."

The following sketch shows the relationship of the slopping site to the upper, outdoor terrace.

A SIMPLE FIRE ESCAPE

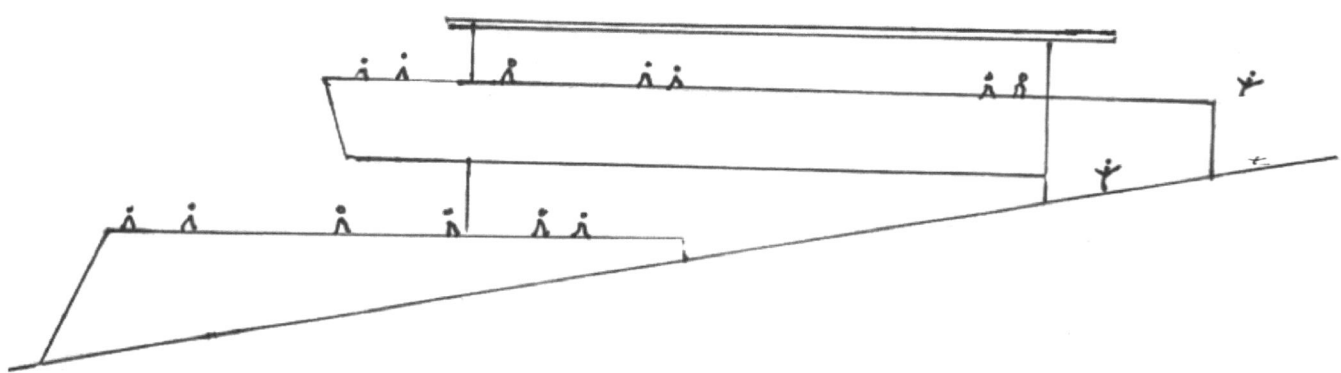

This illustration shows the upper terrace intersecting with the rise in the ground allowing for "any healthy college student can jump off the rear terrace and land safely on his feet."

THE COST PROBLEM

The last, and what proved to be the most critical issue was that of construction costs. When discussing building costs, one must go back in time to the early 1950s. Here are just a few thoughts to set the stage. My Dad had told me at the time that if I could earn $100 per week I would be set for life. When I arrived at Gainesville, the radio played the cattle auctions each day, a movie cost 35¢, and a full steak dinner with hot apple pie and cheddar cheese cost 65¢. The cost of the 1000-seat Annie Pfeiffer Chapel at Florida Southern College, a complicated and integrate masterpiece of the spirit, cost only $100,000 when completed in 1941. As a comparison in 2013 the construction of a Frank Lloyd Wright Visitor's Center, which was built at Florida Southern, a copy of a small Wright home, cost over $2 million dollars.

The original budget for the ZBT House was set by the University at no more than $125,000, but was later increased to $135,000. Mr. Wright had originally estimated that the cost would be $100,000 to $112,000 plus his 10% free. The fraternity had planned to raise 1/5 of the costs, or $22,000, and borrow $89,000 from the Federal Housing and Home Finance Agency under its student dormitory program. This had been discussed originally when I met with the University's Business Manager, George Baughman. That was the plan.

In order to start the fund raising with some self-sacrifice, the fraternity voted to eliminate desserts from its house menu, the savings to go into the building fund. Each brother asked his family for contributions, but with limited results. The fraternity added that they would lower their requirements where needed to lower the cost, but this did not materialize with any significant results.

One of the Fraternity brother's fathers was a large plumbing contractor in South Florida and offered to do all the plumbing at cost, an offer that was never unfortunately incorporated into the final pricing. In addition, one of the fraternity brother's father, manufactured aluminum awning windows in Miami, the center at that time of the aluminum shower door, sliding glass door and window industry. His father said he would donate all the awning windows and Wright was surprisingly receptive. Awning windows were not considered fashionable in elite architectural offices at the time. However,

This rendering of the circular glass wall from the grand living room to the outdoor terrace illustrates Wright's genius. He incorporated the awning windows, shunned by most contemporary architects, in an innovative and creative way as Florida ceiling panels, because they were to be donated by one the father's of the fraternity brothers. This savings was not included in the final bidding process because of its unusual nature.

Wright showed his design genius again by using these awning windows in a wonderful new fashion as full height panels behind the swinging glass doors that formed the long, circular glass wall that fully opened the great Social Living Room onto the Circular Plaza—Florida architecture at its best.

Since I had already graduated and left for the Navy when the bids were let two years later I doubt that these savings were ever remembered or counted into this budget-sensitive project. My guess is they were not.

At the time our fraternity was comparatively new on campus, having only been an active chapter a few years. It had almost no alumni and had no super-rich parents. Added to this was the overriding fact that Frank Lloyd Wright reputation at the time varied between adoration and shame. His architectural work was acclaimed but the newspapers followed him around the world covering his infamous life as a philanderer. Those that did not want to give used this convenient excuse. This was before the era of "celebrity architects" and "ego-architecture." Many of Wright's works at the time been torn down, some abandoned, and many, including some located at Florida Southern, were left without maintenance for long periods of time.

ARCHITECTURAL STUDENTS TO LEARN BY BUILDING

Let us first discuss the question of student participation in the building process which would have resulted in a substantial cost savings. This was a noble goal of both Frank Lloyd Wright and the architectural students like myself at the University who understood the educational and also cost benefits from this type of work. I stated this discussion in a letter of October 25, 1951, when I said "Frank Lloyd Wright accepted the commission on the condition that the School of Architecture participate actively in the construction."

The University's answer was seen in a letter on October 24, 1952, from the fraternity to Wright "…the University stipulates the use of student labor not possible due to local labor conditions," a typical bureaucratic answer from a University without imagination or an understanding of how an architect can supplement his classroom study with actual experience on a real construction site. There was obviously a disconnect between education and administration.

The only exception where University of Florida architectural students actually worked on the project was when Wright wanted a tree survey of the Fraternity House site so he could accommodate the lush tree cover in his design. I, with my classmate Kalvin Platt, who also had been in the group that asked Wright to come to Gainesville, agreed to do a complete site tree survey. Using the topographic map we had gotten for Wright, we spent several days tracking through the dense underbrush and identified, located and sized each tree. We were scratched, sunburned and covered in mite bites that itched for several days after, but we felt we gave him a tool that would influence his design of the site and that involvement with Wright was something we could look back upon and treasure.

Taliesin West, Wright's western home and studio, was built with "tabby" stone walls of fieldstone and mortar with apprentice labor to save cost and to educate architects, an opportunity missed at the University of Florida's School of Architecture during the work on the proposed ZBT fraternity house.

Both at Taliesin West, Frank Lloyd Wright's home and studio in Arizona, and at Wright's Florida Southern College in Lakeland, Florida, (1938–1958) a Methodist liberal arts college, students participated actively in the building process.

Florida Southern was an example of a Wright commission with a lot of desire and little funds to execute. Wright's Florida Southern campus, which was also called "Child of the Sun," is the largest collection of Frank Lloyd Wright architecture in one project in the world. The book *The Fellowship, the Untold Story of Frank Lloyd Wright & the Taliesin Fellowship* states, "…Spivey (Dr. Spivey was president of Florida Southern) had taken Wright's advice: The first three structures at Florida Southern were in fact built by students—though, unlike Wright's apprentices, at least they received a tuition credit for their labor."[4]

The hand-molded blocks, of crushed coquina stone and concrete, had a series of large matching grooves on either side that held thin steel reinforcing bars and mortar. There were no mortar joints on the face of the elongated rectangular blocks and, therefore, the exposed blocks gave a strong horizontal rhythm to the building. Students worked between classes to make these difficult and labor-intensive blocks that added so much to the complete work. Without student labor, the buildings would not have been built.

On my visits to Wright's apprentices at Florida Southern in Lakeland, about three hours travel south of Gainesville, there were several buildings under construction when I visited in the early '50s. So I witnessed students at work. Beside one of the beautiful covered Esplanade walks, there was a machine for the casting of the special concrete blocks, called "tapestry block", which had insets of a rainbow of embedded, tiny chips of colored glass, that gave Wright's campus buildings a jewel-box appearance.

Taliesin West was built primarily with apprentice labor to save on the cost of construction and as a wonderful educational tool. The "tabby" stonewalls composed of selected fieldstone and mortar were an excellent example of the craftsmanship of architectural students.

I used tabby-wall construction in the design of my hotel, the Out Island Inn in Georgetown, *Great Exuma*. Here I used the fieldstone boundary walls that were originally

---

4 *The Fellowship . . .*, Roger Friedland & Harold Zellman, Harper Collins, New York, 2006, pg. 330.

Annie Pfeiffer Chapel, Florida Southern College, Lakeland, Florida

Partially built with student labor, Florida Southern College, Lakeland, Florida. The horizontal lines of the handmade blocks anchor the Florida Southern buildings to the ground, a common design feature of Frank Lloyd Wright. The beauty and fame of Wright's buildings at Florida Southern illustrate the University of Florida's lost opportunity.

Student labor, shunned by the University of Florida, created these jewel-like handcrafted blocks at Florida Southern College in Lakeland, Florida.

laid by slaves for the plantations that were brought to Exuma by the loyalist plantation owners just after the Revolutionary War. In the case of the ZBT house at the University of Florida, the giant circular retaining terrace wall would have been perfect for the use of tabby-wall construction by the student architects. It would have anchored the building to the site, lowered the cost, and would have been an important educational tool for future architects in Florida.

When I visited the construction site of Florida Southern College during my work in 1951 and 1952 with Wright on the fraternity house, I met several times to discuss the ZBT House with both Dr. Ludd M. Spivey, the President of the College, Wright's client and friend, and with Wright's apprentice, Nils Schweizer, who was Wright's representative on the job. He also was to serve as representative of Mr. Wright during construction on the ZBT house. Wright's actual apprentice in charge of the ZBT House was William Wesley Peters.

I remember an anecdotal experience when visiting Florida Southern. The Administration Building was just finished and the President's office was on the second floor. Mr. Wright had designed a reflection pool in the garden outside the building in a little walled garden. As I was talking to Dr. Spivey the sun hit the water and reflected up on the ceiling and then the ripples of the water started radiating on the ceiling. It was beautiful! And I was amazed and said, "how can an architect be that smart to figure out the angle of the sun, where the water is, where the ceiling is and the projection of this light?" (I was told later they paved over this small reflecting pool – so sad.) But I was amazed at the time. So I made the comment and later Dr. Spivey mentioned it to Frank Lloyd Wright. And Frank Lloyd Wright said that it isn't necessarily that he knew of these things, or did these things, but that a good architect and a good building receives a certain amount of surprises by nature. That if you do things right, if you build it right, and you use certain principles, that nice things happen. And that was a nice thing that happened.

I have found in my own architecture that if I do things right, if the building is well designed, there are all kinds of surprises that God gives me back in return.

Another anecdote concerning Florida Southern was told to me by Nils Schweitzer, Wright's apprentice who became my good friend. He said that there was a concrete cantilevered canopy over one of the entrance doors, to keep the rain and the sun off the door. And Nils was very worried that Mr. Wright had designed it too thin, with not enough steel reinforcing. Nils thought that it was going to have a structural problem so he mentioned it to Mr. Wright and Mr. Wright said, "No, it's fine." Nils still was worried so during the construction Nils put extra steel reinforcing in this cantilevered concrete. And when Mr. Wright came to see it on a later visit he said, "wait, look, it's there perfect. There is no problem. Next time I'm going to make it thinner."

I remember at Florida Southern the machine that made the decorative blocks, with beautiful colorful glass chips inserts that were used in the chapel and throughout the various buildings on the campus. The students were taking time, a couple hours a day or so, to build these blocks. This was all donated student labor the concept that we would use to build the ZBT house.

I took a course in surveying as one of the preliminary courses in architecture so with some friends including the late Kalvin Platt we surveyed the property. This was the only work that the architectural student actually did on the project.

The intended site for the ZBT House was beautiful with gorgeous trees, a creek and a hill sloping down towards the street. Luckily, the University was going to put parking on the other side of University Row so there would be no car parking required.

The building was flat and horizontal but the contour was sloped, so that the house ended up with a magnificent, round outdoor Florida terrace.

Mr. Wright designed the building to fit into the natural setting with all the major trees saved. The site was magnificent, the drainage perfect, a creek and beautiful trees and Wright's positioning of the house was perfect, it kept the contour, it married nature — it did all these things.

In a like manner Frank Lloyd Wright said at the very beginning of his acceptance of the commission for the ZBT House, that he wanted architectural students to work on the site to learn by doing while lowering the building cost. Unfortunately, unlike the agreeable and understanding Florida Southern College, the University of Florida said that this would not be permitted. Now 60 years later Florida Southern is honored throughout the world for its Frank Lloyd Wright architecture and the University of Florida is without any architectural significance. The University committee has long been forgotten, scattered to the winds, but their obstructionist decisions has robbed the campus and Florida students of a significant work of architectural history.

AFTER GRADUATION

At this moment in the story's history, June 1953, I graduated from Architecture School and went into the Navy, going directly to Naval Officer's Training School in New Port, Rhode Island. It was during the Korean War. I got married immediately after I graduated from Officer Training School. I then reported for four years of duty on a tanker, the USS Pawcatuck, AO 108. During those four years I was isolated from the world in general and particularly from any connection to the University of Florida and the ZBT/Frank Lloyd Wright house. A tanker is a work ship, seldom in port and when it is, it is anchored out so that a tender is needed to go ashore, weather permitting. When other ships visited ports, we would sail to get them fuel; when other ships took Sundays off, we refueled them; when other ships returned home, we set sail again to get oil and refuel another group of ships.

So my help at the University in navigating the traitorous waters of the ZBT project through the maze of the University committee and the architect was over. I did learn that the Wright house was not built but I did not know why. It was only years later when I visited Taliesin West to record an oral interview of my years with Frank Lloyd Wright that I had access to the files and learned how the story actually ended.

It turns out that after I had left school, the continuing hostility between the University, its Building Committee, now joined by Hollis Rinehart, Chairman of the State Board of Control and Frank Lloyd Wright continued. The conflicts were over building codes, proper drawings and specifications, the special heating, plumbing and electrical work, bidding procedures and costs.

On August 24, 1954, the bids had finally been opened and the bid of M. M. Parrish of Gainesville was the lowest at $165,000.

Wright wrote, "Suggest you get less prejudiced bids and tell us what you are willing to give up." Building a Frank Lloyd Wright building or any quality building of a good, creative architect requires a special contractor, one who can be creative in his methods and costs, unafraid, while being knowledgeable in how to build for an unconventional genius. The various monetary cost savings from the fraternity's parents and the use of architectural student labor were not used.

This marks the tragic end to a once happy story and the glorious opportunity for the University of Florida to gain a degree of architectural significance in history. What followed was a sad tale of lawyers, lawsuits, acrimony, demands for refunds of fees, and self-righteous pronouncements.

The true epilogue to this story was a final judgment entered against Frank Lloyd Wright for $750.

EPITAPH

In a letter dated September 2, 1954, Wright wrote to the University . . . the true sad epitaph to this saga:

"My Dear Official: You and your college must have a queer idea of what constitutes a reputable architect's service. He does not guarantee the cost of his client's desires but does his best with the limitations and the circumstances. Angels can do no more. Not withstanding the unsympathetic attitudes of the college officials increasing delays and adding to costs I have done this. I am sorry that the Fraternity boys and I have met with such interference and it now seems foolish for us all to put more work into this project to further arouse controversy. I have reason to believe the college better pleased if we discontinue our efforts sorry as I am for the fraternity boys."[5]

The Zeta Beta Tau house at the University of Florida

would have been the only university fraternity house designed by FLW in the world.

•

The music swells and the hero dies in the last second of the last act and the curtain silently draws closed.

---

[5] "FLW's Other Florida Designs," Randolph C. Henning, *Frank Lloyd Wright Quarterly*, Winter 2–2, FLW Foundation, Taliesin West, Scotsdale, AZ, page 17.

PART IV — RENDERINGS OF THE ZETA BETA TAU HOUSE BY FRANK LLOYD WRIGHT AT THE UNIVERSITY OF FLORIDA

Renderings by Jeffrey Baker:
Architect, Albany, New York

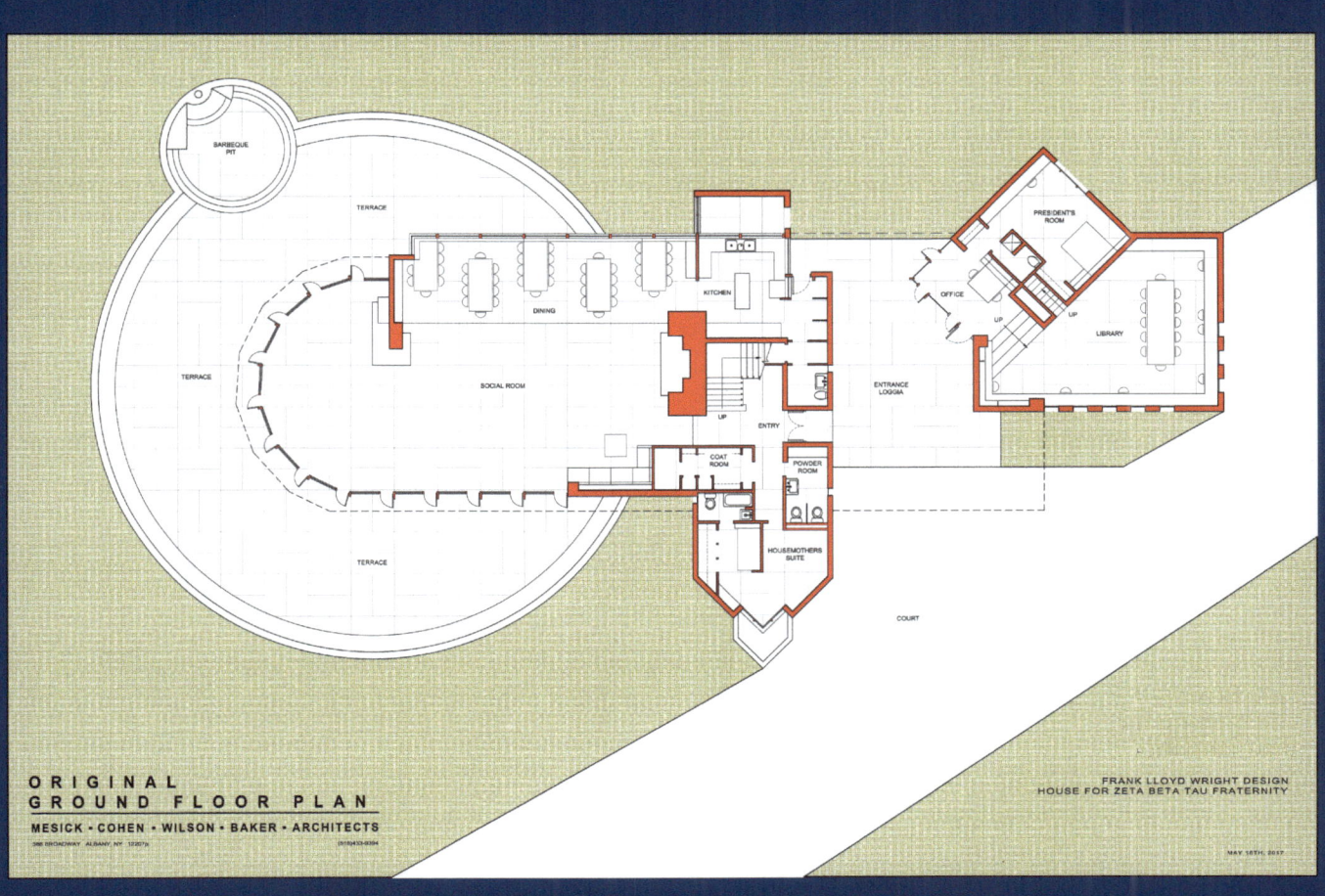

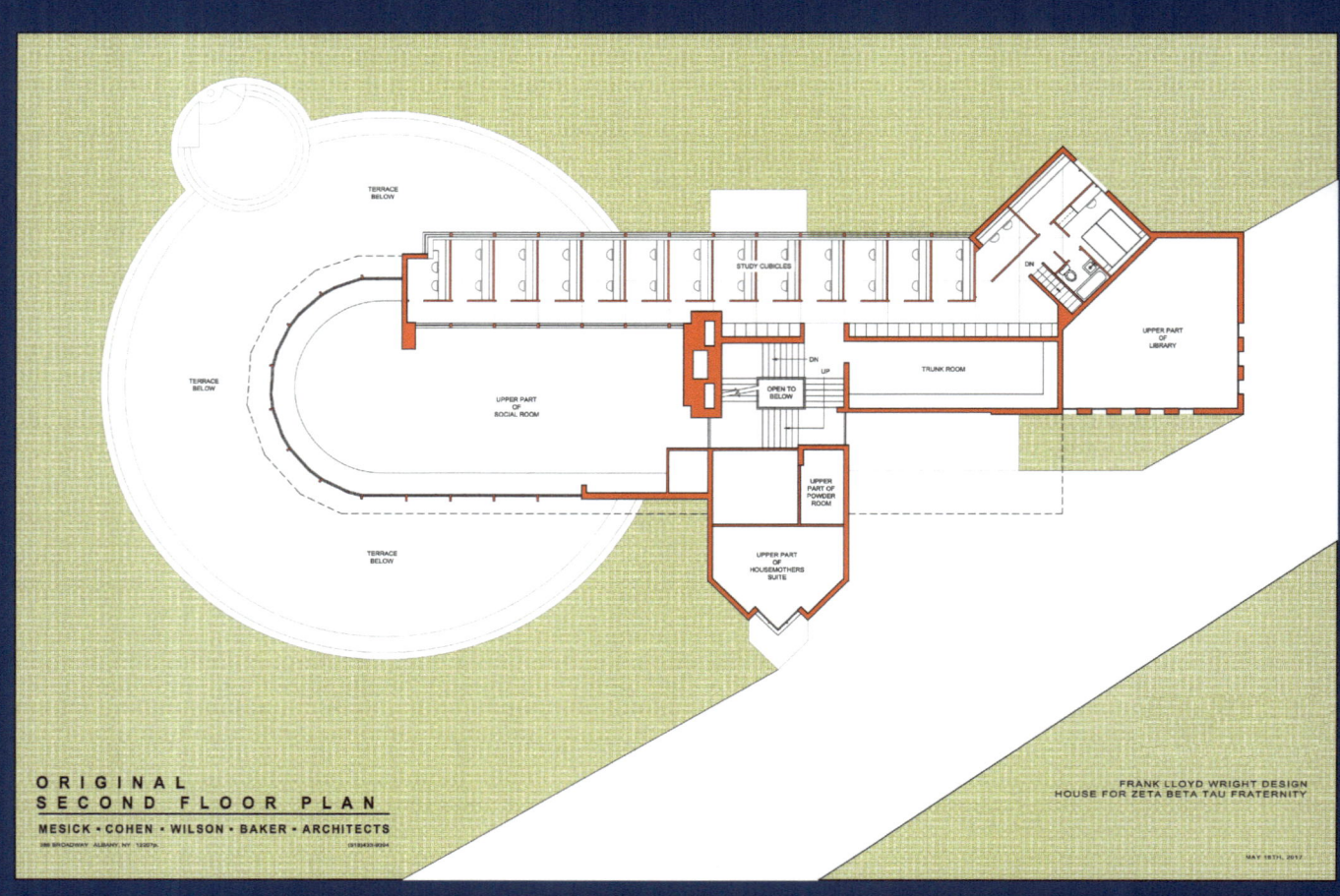

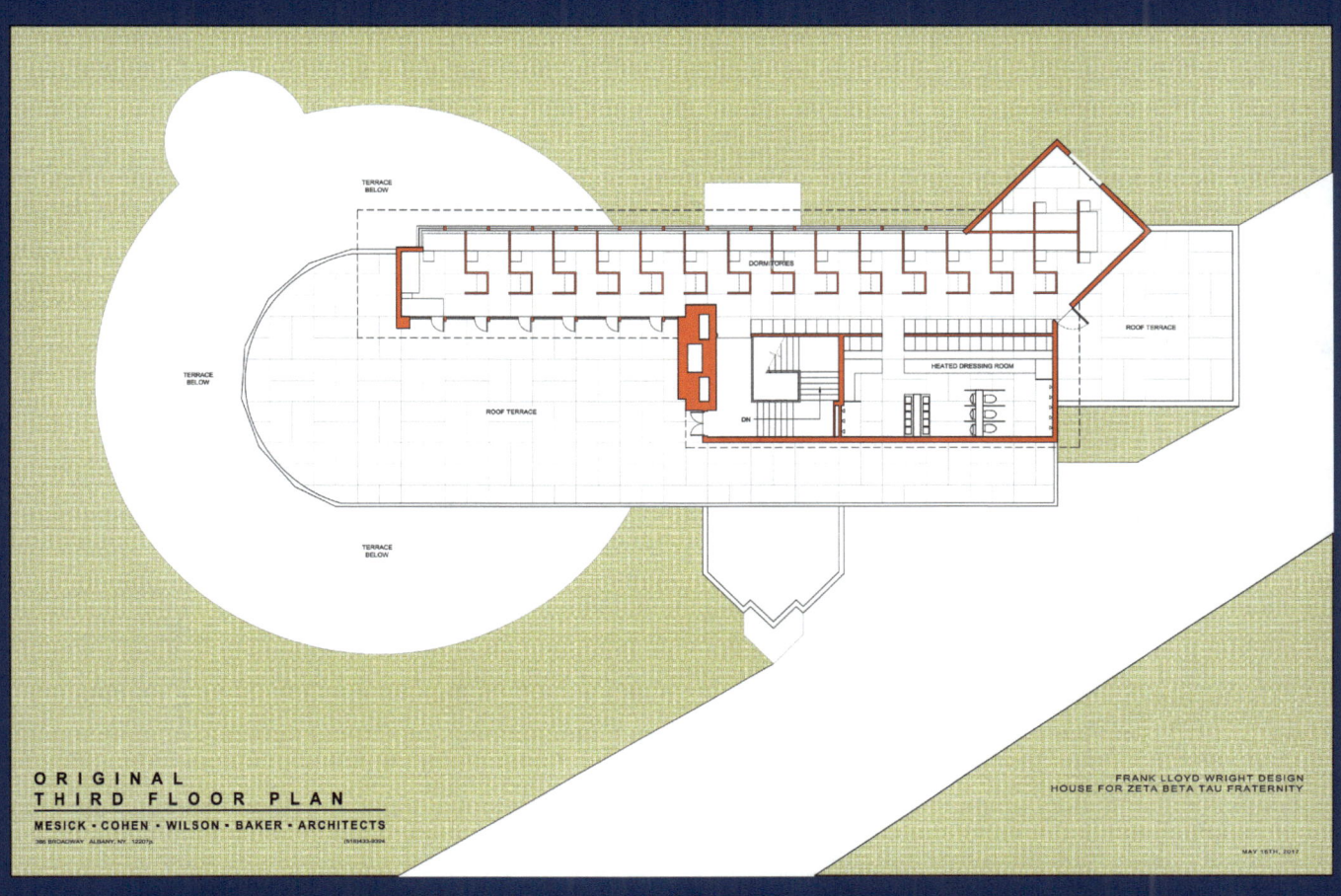

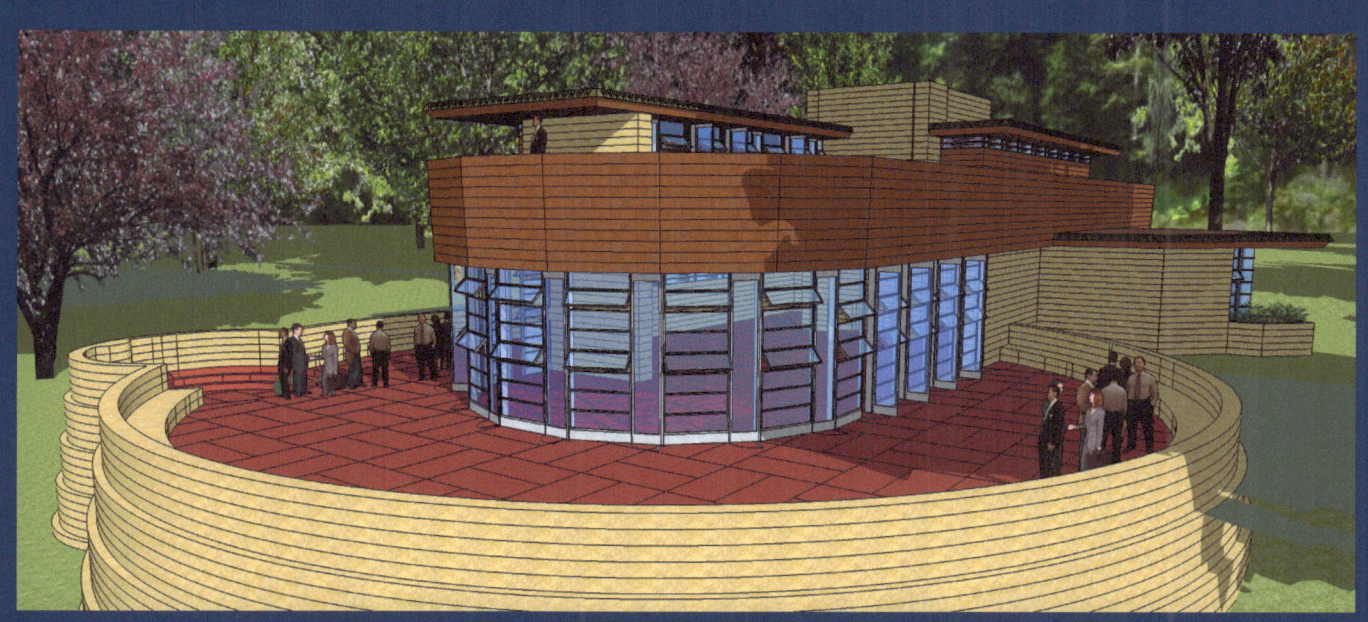

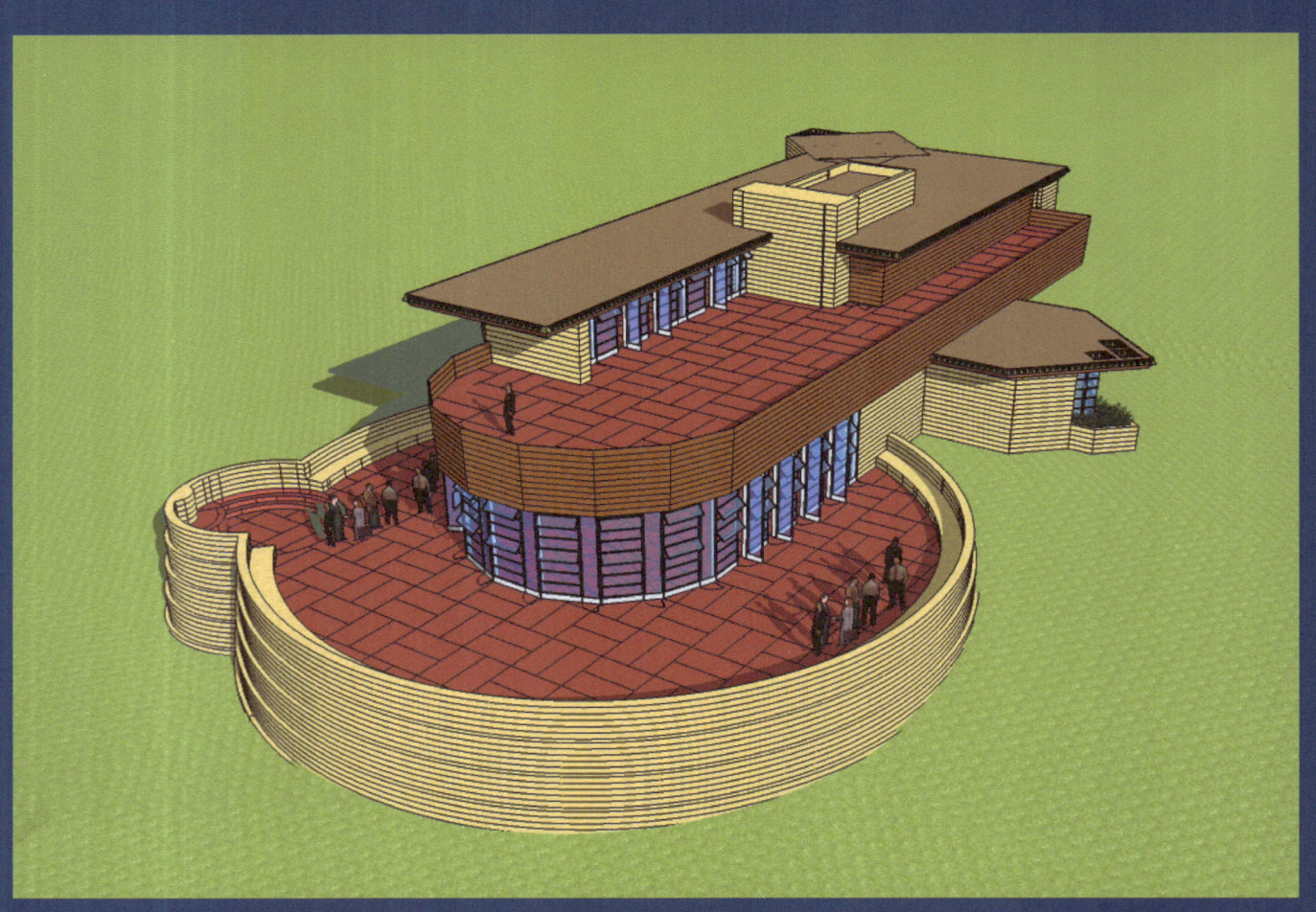

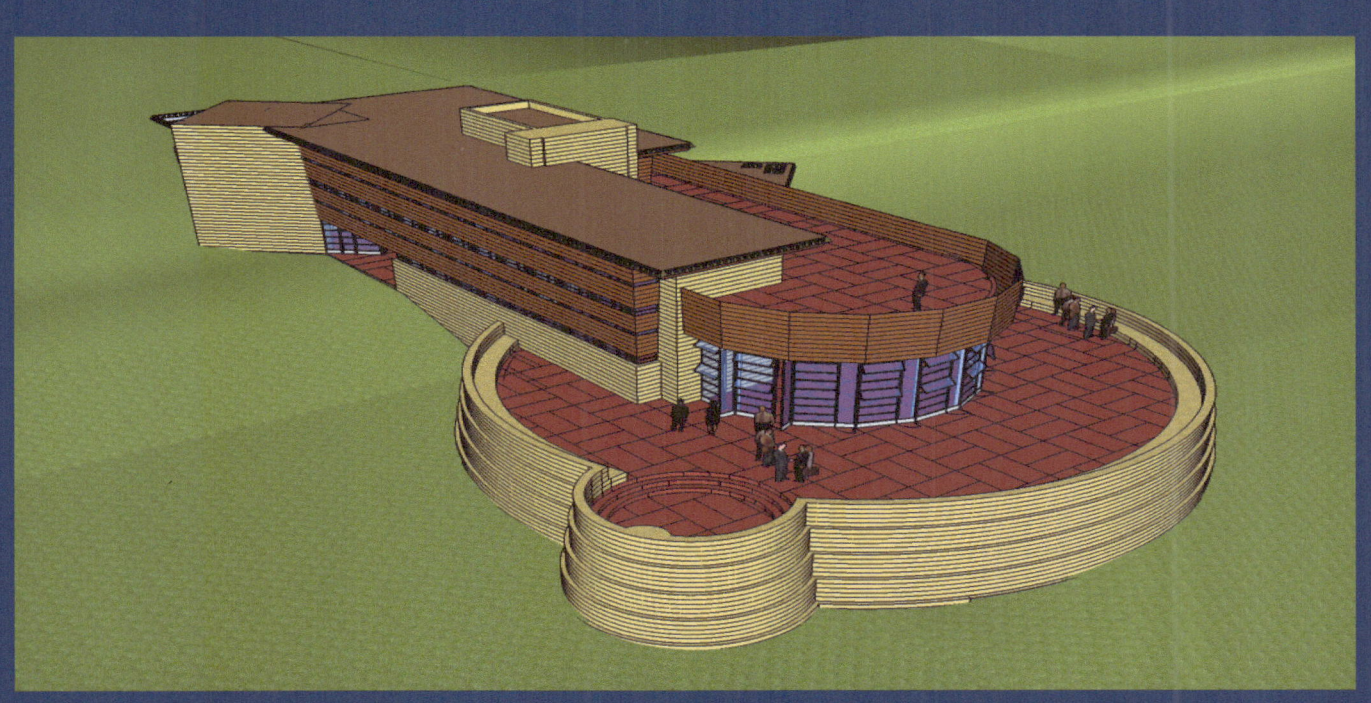

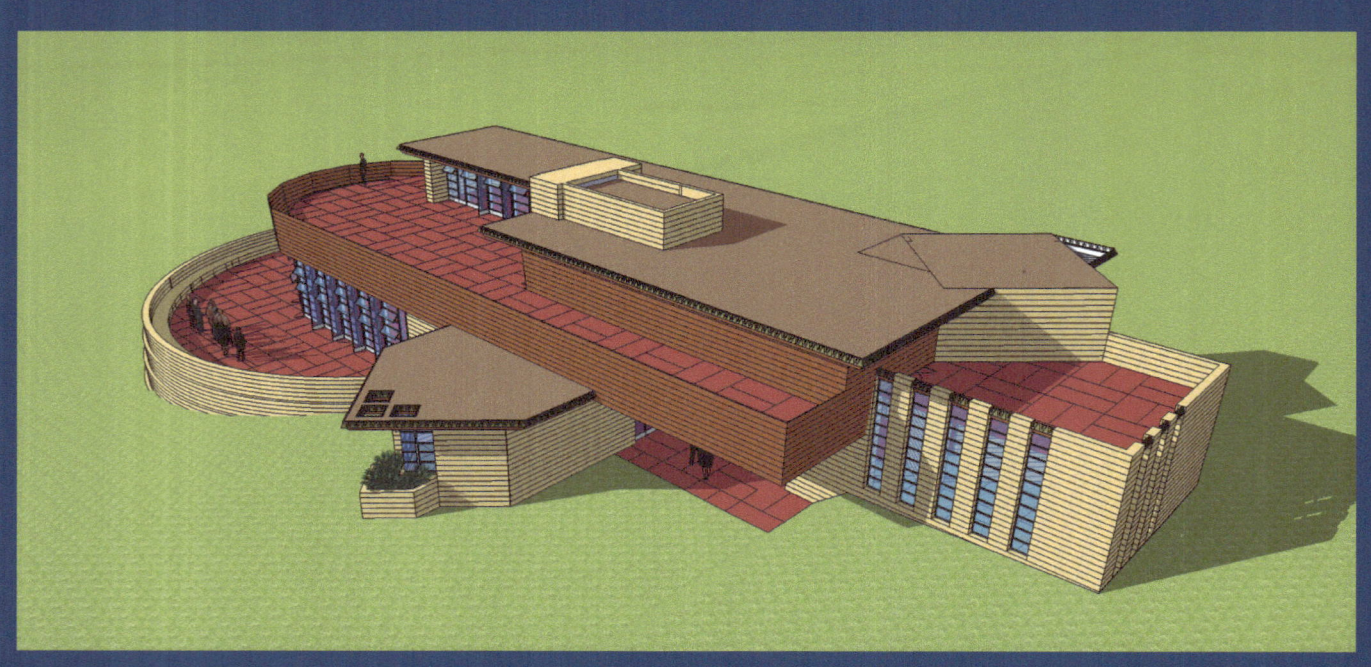

APPENDIX

Architectural Elevations, Letters from the author
to Frank Lloyd Wright starting with one dated
October 25, 1951, just two days after the lecture,
Architectural Plans and Elevations,
Newspaper articles on the FLW lecture at UF

and

Photograph of the Zeta Beta Tau fraternity brothers in 1951
at the time of their work with Frank Lloyd Wright

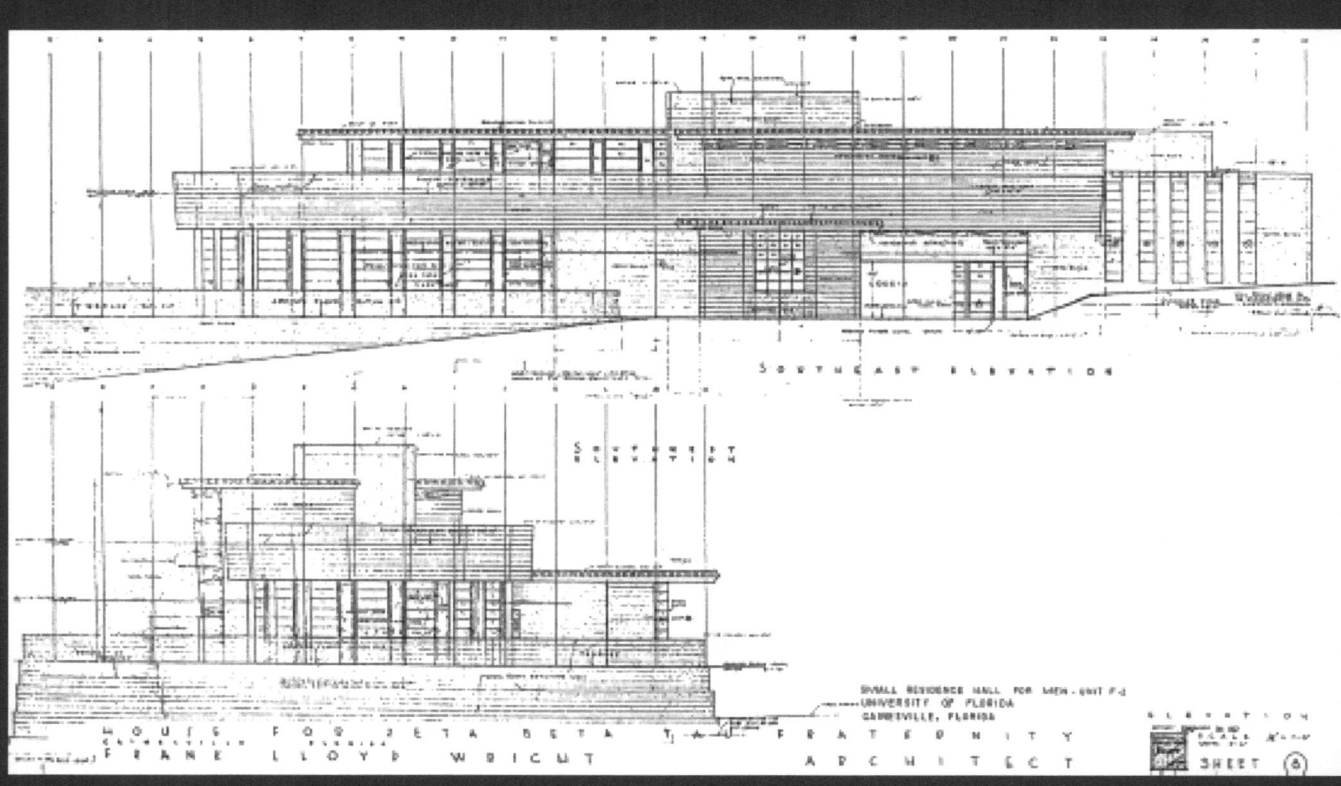

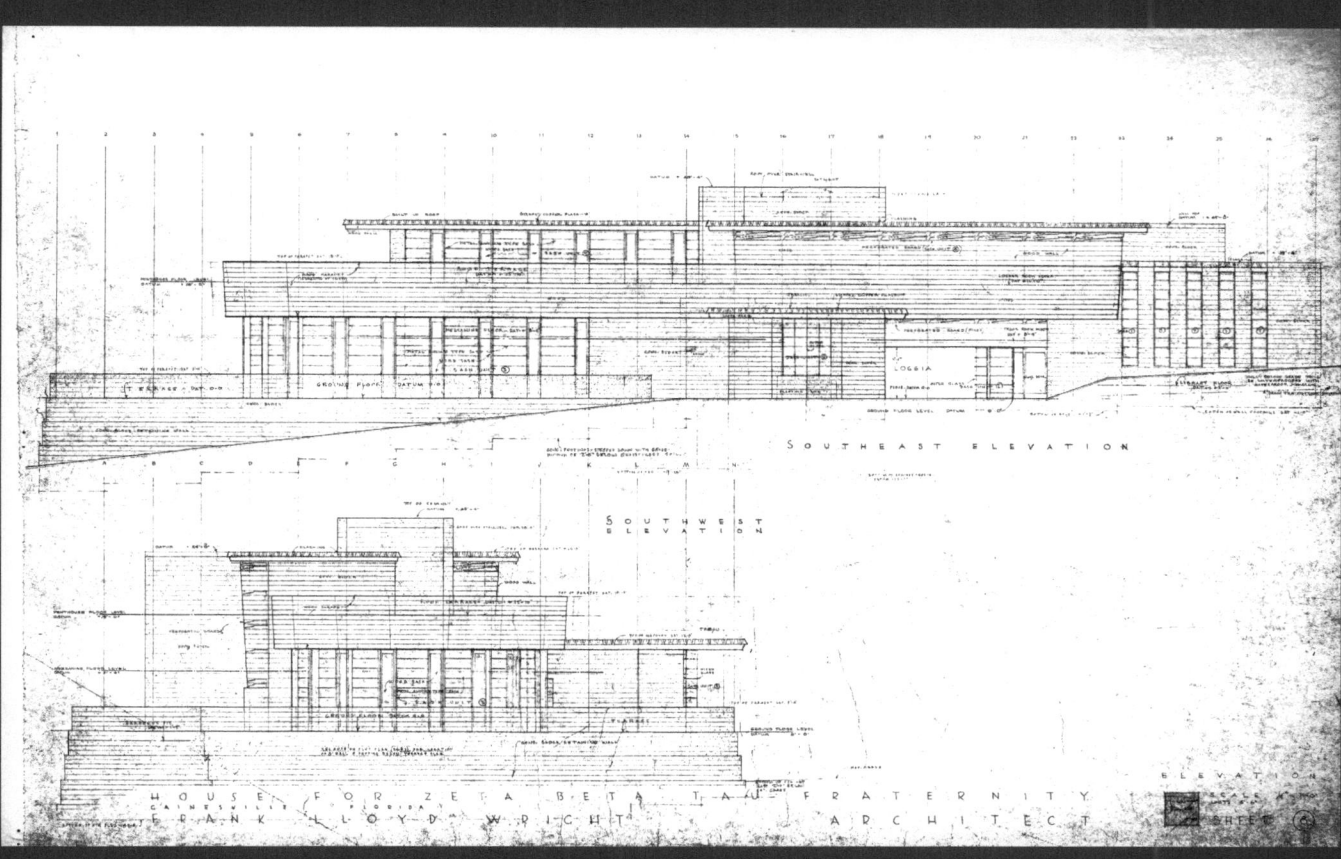

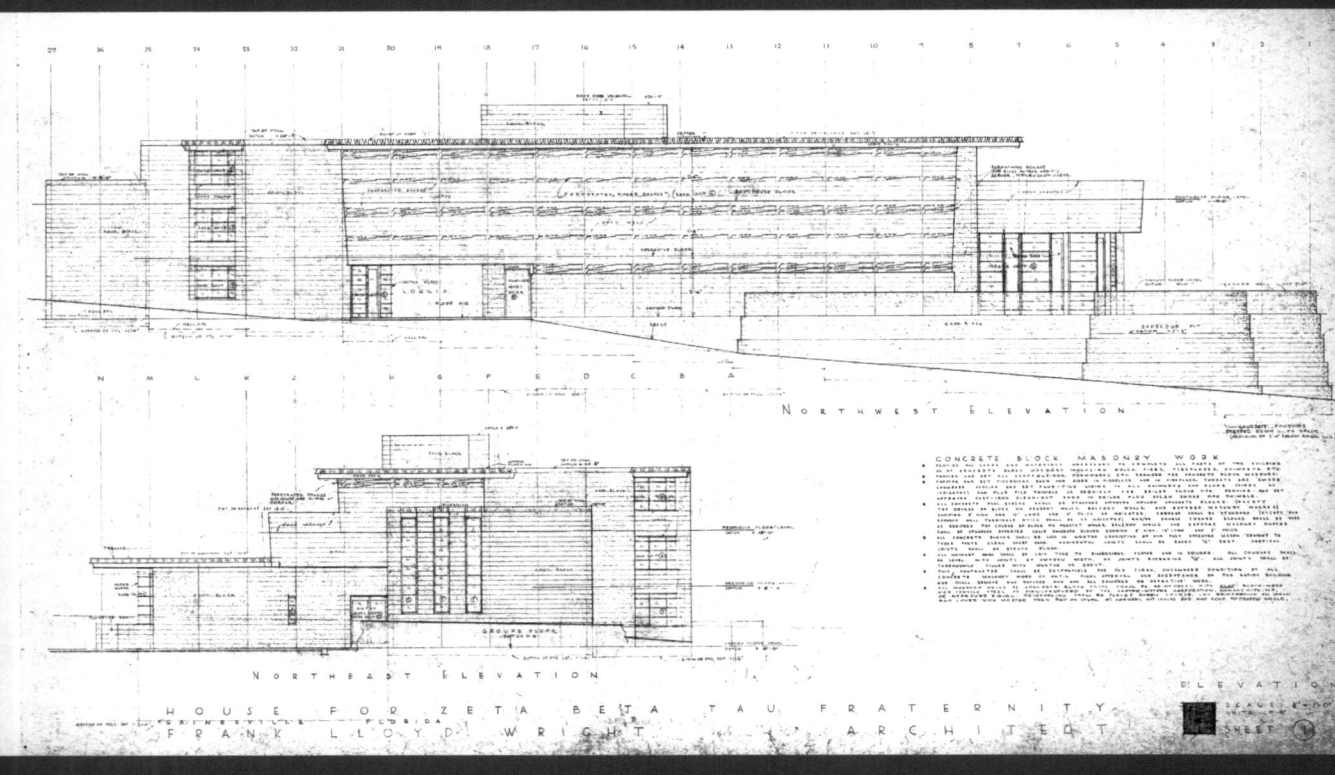

Alpha Zeta Chapter

Zeta Beta Tau Fraternity

BOX 2656, UNIVERSITY STATION
GAINESVILLE, FLORIDA

October 25, 1951

Mr. Eugene Masselink
Taliesen Fellowship
Spring Green
Wisconsin

Dear Mr. Masselink

In conjunction with a verbal agreement made by Mr. Wright, on October 23, 1951, to design a local home for the Zeta Beta Tau Fraternity, on the University of Florida's campus, I would like to get some idea as to the information that we should send, in addition to that which is to be mailed at his request in the near future. (topographic map and pictures of site)

His acceptance of this project , on the condition that students from our school of architecture participate actively in the construction, leaves me in the position of having to present some information as to the building proceidure to both the fraternity and the interested students before we can go agead with this arrangment. If you could give me some idea of what Mr. Wright has in mind in this respect I could start making definate commitments to the parties involved.

I would also like to have some idea of probable contract agreements, including financial arrangments, time schedules and other building arrangments.

As an architectural student and as chairman of the Building Committee of the fraternity, I believe you can understand my eagerness to begin negotiations for this type of project. I hope you will express, to Mr. Wright, the students appreeiation for this opportunity, as we wish to do as soon as he himself can be contacted.

Sincerely,

Kenneth Treister

Kenneth Treister

Alpha Zeta Chapter
Zeta Beta Tau Fraternity

BX 2656, UNIVERSITY STATION
GAINESVILLE, FLORIDA

November 1, 1951

Mr. Frank Lloyd Wright
Spring Green,
Wisconsin

Dear Mr. Wright:

    As a portion of the material you requested in reguard to designing a home for our local ZBT chapter on campus, I am sending what information we have been able to collect thus far. I hope that this can give you some idea of the general site, as it is in a condition before the rest of the area is developed.

    Your secretary was contacted on October 25 in an attempt to begin making arrangements for putting the project on a student working basis. As you are now more likely to be through with your immediate traveling we would like to get started with the compiling of the necessary information that you would need for the design.

    As soon as possible we will send additional pictures that are not so subject to weather conditions and a list of the functions the house would have to perform as a residence fo 40 boys out of a membership of 60. The map we do not feel to be entirely accurate in contour and placement of trees. I have arranged to make a survey of the site as a project as soon as possible in connection with our student study in surveying. If that would be suffisently acceptable to you we would be glad to forward our results as an indication of the site at a better scale.

    Your interest in the design has not been mentioned to the entire fraternity and only a few in the school of architecture have any knowledge of the idea. I had thought it better to wait until something definite could be said, as I have no doubt of the interest that will be shown when the complete program is presented.

Alpha Zeta Chapter
Zeta Beta Tau Fraternity

P. O. BOX 2686, UNIVERSITY STATION
GAINESVILLE, FLORIDA

The financing will have to be made in the near future and for this we will have to have some definite statement to present to the authorities for conformation. There was pressure on the Building Committee to have the plans in the near future but I am sure that with your commission there would not be that time restriction.

We had planned to build a home that will cost about $100,000. The University has put a limit of $125,000. on all construction in the new area.

As students we are especially interested to know of the part we are to preform in the building of your design. You can be assured that the students will value the experience as a significant part of their education and as an indication of an attitude that could be a guidepost for the school to follow.

Sincerely,

Kenneth Treister
Chairman, Building Committee
Zeta Beta Tau Fraternity
University of Florida

Alpha Zeta Chapter

Zeta Beta Tau Fraternity

P. O. BOX 2656, UNIVERSITY STATION
GAINESVILLE, FLORIDA

November 14th, 1951

Mr. Eugene Masselink
Secretary to Frank Lloyd Wright
Taliesen
Spring Green
Wisconsin

Dear Mr. Masselink:

I received you letter of November 3rd, and in accord with your request I will send you in the near future an accurate survey of the property, additional pictures, and a complete list of the Fraternity's requirements.

The Trustees of the Fraternity have requested that, as soon as ossible a contractorial agreement, between the architect and ourselves, be in our files. This is so we can announce our architect in conjuction with our building fund drive. I will be in Miami Beach, Fla. after the 16th and would appreciate it if you would send the contract to me.

Mr. Kenneth Treister
1220 Lenox Avenue
Miami Beach, Florida

Sincerely yours,

Kenneth Treister

X018 1307 11/28/51

Alpha Zeta Chapter
Zeta Beta Tau Fraternity
November 28, 1951

BOX 2656, UNIVERSITY STATION
GAINESVILLE, FLORIDA

Mr. Kenneth Treister
Box 2656, University Station
Gainesville
Florida

Mr. Frank Lloyd Wright
Taliesin Fellowship
Spring Green
Wisconsin

Dear Mr. Wright:

As you requested I am inclosing a list of the Fraternity's requirements for our new home, and in a separate cylendar an accurate survey of the property.

We hope that the requirements we listed are complete. However they are only tenetive and we welcome any suggestions or comments that you fell are necessary. Some Items may be obvious but were included to assure complete understanding.

For this project we have the necessary restriction of $110,000 for the completed expenditure. Some of the requirements are dependent upon your decisions as to distribution of funds for their inclusion. We have in the chapter a number of men who's fathers are in the building industry. We can therefore count on a reduction in the cost of some building materials, electrical work, all plumming materials, and possibly furniture.

We hope to hear from you in the near future not only on the actual fraternity house design but as to what part we as architectural students will play in the project.

Sincerely

X02/C02 8/18/52

1220 Lenox Ave.
Miami Beach Fla.
Aug. 18, 1952

Mr. Eugene Masselink
Secretary to Frank Lloyd Wright
Taliesin
Spring Green
Wisconsin

Dear Mr. Masselingk:

Received the preliminary plans and we are extremely
 pleased with them.

Please send me your approximate estimate of the
 building costs of our new home, exclusive of
furnishings, immediatly, so that we can submit same
to our National Officiers and University Officials
in Jax. on the 25th of Aug.

            Sincerely yours,

            Kenneth Treister
            Kenneth Treister

Wright delights, shocks audience in Atlanta talk

ATLANTA — Frank Lloyd Wright, the snappy, 82-year-old dean of modern architecture, both delighted and shocked a large audience at Georgia Tech last night.

The philosophical discussion of the 82-year-old Wright touched, at times, only vaguely on architecture and often had more bite than design.

He dubbed designing as the blind spot in American culture and added that we know a great deal more about everything else than we do about it.

"All you need as proof," he said, is to look at the buildings in which our educational campaigns are carried out."

Then he touched on politics, the state of the world, capitalism, the "newly rich", the United Nations and education.

Of the latter he said simply: "Education has not been on speaking terms with culture for a long time."

On the American people as a whole: "They sit behind the wheel of their car with a cigar cocked at 45 degrees and their hat pulled down over their eyes thinking they're 125 horsepower."

And finally of American architecture: "We've got the kind of architecture we deserve. We did it. It wasn't done to us. We just didn't know any better."

Wright to talk here tonight

Frank Lloyd Wright is well known throughout the country for his impromptu speeches covering a wide variety of subjects, and the 82-year-old father of modern architecture is expected to deliver one of those talks here tonight.

Wright is appearing at the University of Florida under the sponsorship of the student chapter of the American Institute of Architects. He will speak in the University gymnasium at 8 p.m.

Speeches by Wright, which are rare occasions, cover a wide variety of subjects ranging from music and cookery to posing for photographers. His "off-the-cuff" style of delivery usually keeps his audience well amused, and sometimes confused, but always entertained.

Wright is the famed designer of some of the most controversial architectural projects throughout the world. The foremost example of his style of design in Florida is Florida Southern College at Lakeland. He also designed the ultra-modern Johnson Wax Co. plant and the Imperial Hotel in Tokyo.

Congress may sidestep vote on Gen. Clark

WASHINGTON *P — Opposition by Senator Connally (D-Texas) gave weight today to a Democratic move to avoid a vote on President Truman's nomination of Gen. Mark Clark as ambassador to the Vatican.

Connally based his fight

WRIGHT DECLARES

Europeans look upon U.S. as 'dollar imperialists'

By Jim Camp

People in other countries think of the United States as a nation of "dollar imperialists," famed Architect Frank Lloyd Wright said last night.

Speaking before an attentive audience of around 5,000 in Florida Gymnasium, the "father of American architecture" pointed out that those abroad don't like the Marshall Plan.

"They think it is a scheme to buy Europe away from the Communists," Wright said, basing his conclusions on personal observations during a recent trip overseas.

"They resent the fact that we think they can be bought—but they took our money!" the salty, 81-year-old proponent of "organic architecture" stated.

Defining organic architecture as "living, natural architecture," Wright simplified its meaning by pointing out that organic "things" are the only "living things."

"Buildings should have a significance," he said. "They should mean something, and say it."

The South, Wright insisted, can go straight to organic architecture, if we will rid ourselves of "Colonial" styling and other sentimentalities.

Colonial architecture was dismissed as "bastardized Greek." Following the Civil War, the speaker reminded, the South did not go in for other such "extravagances" as skyscrapers, which he said will eventually have to be torn down.

In spite of all their opportunities, Americans have developed no culture of their own, Wright said, but have remained a nation of imitators. Our "style" of architecture, he added, has been the "blind spot" on any sort of culture we may have attempted.

Cultural development, according to Wright, must now come from the homes of the people—the democratic family unit—since education "hasn't waked up."

"De-centralization will be the salvation of the nation, if it is to have a culture of its own," Wright stated. "We point to our skyscrapers with the greatest pride, yet the country is the best place to build a skyscraper.

"The Russians know this."

The American unions have
Continued On Page FIVE

Wright

Continued from Page One

put the country on the assembly line "for keeps," Wright pointed out, but they must be made to realize that they can't kill off apprenticeship and live.

"We must do something about it," he warned, "or we will have a 'machine architecture' of prefabrication, home-wiring and other things we are being driven to by the unions."

Stressing the need of a good atmosphere in which to live, Wright said the pursuit of the beautiful is the only pursuit of America, as a democracy, that is worth a man's time.

"All the fine words in our language have been sold down the river by the advertising agencies," stated Wright. He challenged anyone in the audience to state his chief interest in life, as an American.

When someone expressed a desire to be able to "think freely," Wright attacked by asking, "How about 'living' freely?" to spontaneous applause. Of the "Four Freedoms," the speaker charged that if America has to count its freedoms by fours, then we don't really have freedom.

Comparing government to architecture in a structural sense, Wright said that if we do not have a good structure of government then we can't live happily. "We must get the idea over to Americans that we are somebody in our right," he insisted.

Declaring frankly that "architecture is in a worse pickle than painting," Wright went on to say that sculpture, as a great art, has disappeared from the face of the earth.

"Music is the only one of the great arts remaining," the architect said, "and that is because it is still modern, having been based upon instruments that we continue to use.

Renewing his attack on Colonial building, Wright explained that people tend to love this kind of thing because they refuse to live in the present—which, he said, has more to offer.

Organic architecture, he said, still refusing to give ground to any other style, produces buildings which become part of their surroundings.

"You don't have to go to a little hole in the wall to see them, either!" he pointed out.

Frank Lloyd Wright (left), one
president of the Student Chapter
Wright was heard in a lecture las

States' Rights Return Urged By Architect

Frank Lloyd Wright Raps Unionism, Centralizing of Government

Times-Union Bureau

GAINESVILLE, Oct. 23—In a speech on the University of Florida campus tonight, the "father of modern architecture," Frank Lloyd Wright, advocated the return of states' rights and decentralization of government, and at the same time hit at unionism and the nation's educational system.

In calling for States' rights, he said democracy needs sound structure in Government, that the Constitution was such an organic structure but has constantly been changed by having things taken away from it.

Wright said the Russians seem to have learned the secret of decentralization—that "a culture of our own will never come from the city."

He deplored the fact that the unions in America have thrown the trades out of line and has put itself on the assembly line by limiting apprenticeship.

The 81-year-old architect stated "we have no culture in this country. It is up to the young architect to change this, since the environment in which we live is the very basis for a culture.

"Neither is education doing anything about it. It will have to come from the family at home," he told a large crowd at Florida Gymnasium.

An advocate of organic architecture over the colonial type, Wright said the South can go straight to organic architecture because it was defeated in the Civil War and did not go in for "such extravagances like skyscrapers which will have to be torn down."

He also gave a boost to Dr. Ludd M. Spivey, president of Florida Southern College, who was in attendance tonight. Wright said the FSC campus was an attempt at an organic architecture for the young.

Wright himself designed many of the buildings on the Florida Southern campus.

ZBT Fraternity brothers 1951, at the time of the Frank Lloyd Wright design proposal.